MHRA STYLE GUIDE

A HANDBOOK FOR AUTHORS, EDITORS, AND WRITERS OF THESES

LONDON

MODERN HUMANITIES RESEARCH ASSOCIATION

2002

This *Style Guide* is the successor to the *MHRA Style Book* first published in 1971 under the editorship of A. S. Maney and R. L. Smallwood and revised in later editions (fifth edition, 1996). It has been edited by a subcommittee of the MHRA consisting of Glanville Price (Chairman), Malcolm Cook, Michael Gallico, Gerard Lowe, Martin McLaughlin, Stephen Parkinson, and Liz Rosindale.

Copies may be ordered from Subscriptions Department, Maney Publishing, Hudson Road, Leeds LS9 7DL, UK (e-mail maney@maney.co.uk).

The *Style Guide* is available online at the MHRA's website (www.mhra.org.uk).

For further information about individual membership and the activities of the MHRA, or to access the *Style Guide* online, visit the website at www.mhra.org.uk or contact the Honorary Secretary, Dr David Gillespie, Department of European Studies and Modern Languages, University of Bath, Bath BA2 7AY, UK (e-mail mlsdcg@bath.ac.uk).

ISBN 0-947623-62-0

Reprinted in 2004

© Modern Humanities Research Association, 2002

Produced by Maney Publishing, Leeds, UK

CONTENTS

INTRODUCTION   I

I   PREPARING MATERIAL FOR PUBLICATION

1.1   Introduction   2
1.2   General   2
      1.2.1   Preferred Styles   2
      1.2.2   Submission on Disk or as an E-mail Attachment   3
      1.2.3   Checking   3
1.3   Preparation of Copy   3
      1.3.1   General   3
      1.3.2   Instructions for the Typing of Copy   4
              1.3.2.1   General   4
              1.3.2.2   Corrections, Insertions, and Comments   4
      1.3.3   Founts and Capitals   4
      1.3.4   Headings and Subdivisions   5
      1.3.5   Dashes   5
      1.3.6   Quotation Marks   6
      1.3.7   Running Heads   6
      1.3.8   Numbering of Pages   6
      1.3.9   Typing Conventions   6
      1.3.10 Special Characters and Diacritics, and Non-Latin
              Scripts   7
      1.3.11 Notes   7
      1.3.12 Illustrations   8
      1.3.13 Tables   9
      1.3.14 Cross-references   9
      1.3.15 Copy Produced on a Typewriter   9

1.4	Author-typeset Formats	9
1.4.1	General	9
1.4.2	Camera-ready Copy	10
1.4.2.1	General	10
1.4.2.2	Typographic Style	10
1.4.2.3	Presentation of CRC	10
1.4.3	Direct Electronic Submission	10
1.5	Order of Parts of a Book	10

2 SPELLING

2.1	Preferred Spellings	12
2.2	Diacritics	12
2.3	Hyphens	13
2.4	Quotations	14
2.5	The Possessive	14
2.6	Place Names	15
2.7	Personal Names	15
2.8	Slavonic Names	16

3 ABBREVIATIONS

3.1	General	17
3.2	Titles	17
3.3	In Footnotes and Endnotes	17
3.4	Use of Full Point	18
3.5	Truncations	18
3.6	American States	18

4 PUNCTUATION

4.1	Commas	20
4.2	Dashes	20
4.3	Parentheses and Brackets	20
4.4	Punctuation in Headings	21
4.5	Punctuation with Italics	21
4.6	Quotation Marks	22

4.7	Exclamation Marks	22
4.8	Ellipses	22

5 CAPITALS

5.1	General	23
5.2	Titles and Dignities	23
5.3	Movements and Periods	24
5.4	Titles of Books and Other Writings	24
5.5	Hyphenated Compounds	26
5.5.1	Titles and Headings	26
5.5.2	In the Body of the Text	26
5.6	Accented Capitals	26
5.7	Small Capitals	27

6 ITALICS

6.1	General	28
6.2	Foreign Words and Quotations	28
6.3	Titles of Books and Other Writings	29
6.4	Titles of Films, Musical Compositions, and Works of Art	29

7 DATES, NUMBERS, CURRENCY, AND WEIGHTS AND MEASURES

7.1	Dates	30
7.2	Numbers	30
7.3	Roman Numerals	31
7.4	Currency	31
7.5	Weights and Measures	32

8 QUOTATIONS AND QUOTATION MARKS

8.1	General	34
8.2	In Languages Other than English	34
8.3	Short Quotations	34
8.4	Long Quotations	35
8.5	Quotations from Plays	36

8.6	Omissions	37
8.7	Copyright	38

9   FOOTNOTES AND ENDNOTES

9.1	General	39
9.2	Methods of Limiting Notes	39
9.3	Position and Numbering	39

10   REFERENCES

10.1	General	41
10.2	Forms of Reference	41
	10.2.1 General	41
	10.2.2 Books	42
	10.2.3 Chapters or Articles in Books	45
	10.2.4 Articles in Journals	47
	10.2.5 Articles in Newspapers and Magazines	48
	10.2.6 Theses and Dissertations	49
	10.2.7 Plays and Long Poems	49
	10.2.8 The Bible	50
	10.2.9 Manuscripts	50
	10.2.10 Online Publications	51
	10.2.10.1 General	51
	10.2.10.2 Online Articles	51
	10.2.10.3 Online Databases	52
	10.2.10.4 Other Sources	52
	10.2.11 Recordings, Films, and Digital Media	52
10.3	Later References	53
10.4	Citation by the Author–Date System	54
10.5	Cross-references	55
10.6	Bibliographies	56

11   PREPARATION OF INDEXES

11.1	General	58
11.2	Index Entries	58
11.3	The Indexer	59

12 PREPARATION OF THESES AND DISSERTATIONS

12.1	General	60
12.2	Length of the Thesis	60
12.3	Parts of the Thesis	60
	12.3.1 Title Page	60
	12.3.2 Abstract or Synopsis	61
	12.3.3 Table of Contents and List of Illustrations	61
	12.3.4 Preface, Acknowledgements, Declaration	61
	12.3.5 List of Abbreviations	61
	12.3.6 Text	62
	12.3.7 Notes	62
	12.3.8 Appendices	62
	12.3.9 Bibliography	62
	12.3.10 Index	63
12.4	Preparation of the Final Typescript	63
	12.4.1 General	63
	12.4.2 Paper, Typeface, and Margins	63
	12.4.3 Spacing	63
	12.4.4 Pagination	64
	12.4.5 Headings and Subheadings	64
	12.4.6 Checking and Correction	64
	12.4.7 Cross-references	64
	12.4.8 Illustrations and Tables	64
	12.4.9 Number of Copies	65
12.5	Binding	65
12.6	Permission to Consult and Copy	65
12.7	Further Reading	65

13 USEFUL WORKS OF REFERENCE — 66

14 PROOF CORRECTION — 67

15 INDEX — 78

INTRODUCTION

This *Style Guide* derives from and replaces the *MHRA Style Book*, edited by A. S. Maney and R. L. Smallwood, which was first published in 1971 with the stated aim of helping authors and editors of academic publications and those preparing theses 'to achieve clarity and consistency in matters of style and presentation'. In later editions edited by subcommittees of the MHRA (the fifth and last was published in 1996), the *Style Book* was progressively revised and expanded.

This *Style Guide*, like its predecessor, is primarily intended for use in connection with MHRA's own publications, both books and periodicals. However, our *Style Book* has been adopted by growing numbers of other authors, editors, and publishers and, in recent editions and yet more so in the present *Style Guide*, account is taken of comments, suggestions, and representations made by other users. Any further comments and suggestions for amendments or additions that might be incorporated in future are welcomed and may be sent to the e-mail address given below.

Users of the *Style Book* will notice two major omissions in this *Style Guide*. Since many journals, including some of those published by the MHRA, have, for good reasons, adopted conventions on the presentation of book reviews that differ from those recommended in the chapter on 'Preparation of book reviews', it was felt that that chapter had outlived its usefulness and editors of MHRA journals, and doubtless others, will in future produce their own style sheets. It was also felt that the majority of the terms included in the 'Glossary' provided in all editions of the *Style Book* except the first were of relevance to publishers and printers rather than to writers and editors and could therefore be dispensed with, the more so since unfamiliar technical terms can be looked up in *The Oxford Dictionary for Writers and Editors*, 2nd edn (Oxford: Oxford University Press, 2000).

Electronic versions of this *Style Guide* are also available. Further information, including details of latest revisions and updates, may be obtained from http://www.mhra.org.uk or mail@mhra.org.uk.

PREPARING MATERIAL FOR PUBLICATION

1.1 INTRODUCTION

This chapter is concerned with the preparation of copy for editing and subsequent publication in any medium. Many of its principles also hold for the form in which articles are submitted for consideration by journal editors (see 1.2.1). Submission of copy prepared using a word processor has become accepted practice, whereas copy prepared using a typewriter has become the exception. This chapter is therefore written on the assumption that the reader will be using a word processor, although specific guidelines are provided for those using a typewriter. In this chapter, 'typed' means 'prepared on a keyboard' (not necessarily on a typewriter) and 'typescript' refers to any form of hard copy produced in this way.

Most publishers now require authors to supply copy on disk in word processor format and some no longer accept copy solely as typescript. Few editors (and certainly none of the MHRA editors) will now accept hand-written copy.

1.2 GENERAL

1.2.1 Preferred Styles

When preparing a text for publication, the author should take due account of the 'Notes for Contributors' or 'Instructions to Authors' of the journal or series. These will specify the form in which articles or book typescripts should be submitted for consideration, and the organization of copy in articles for publication (such as the positioning of abstracts and details of the author's affiliation). While some publications have their own style books or style sheets, most base their 'Notes' on a common guide to style such as this *Style Guide*, with additional specific requirements depending on the preference of their editors, publisher, or printer. Contributors to the MHRA publications *The Slavonic and East European Review* and *The Year's Work in Modern Language Studies* should note that each of these has certain conventions that differ somewhat from those laid down in this *Style Guide* and which must be strictly observed.

If your text incorporates material received from other authors, ensure that it conforms in every detail to your own layout.

Once a text has been accepted for publication, editors will normally ask the author to prepare a final revised version of the text, including corrections to the style of the work, in addition to any substantive revisions recommended by readers. As a further safeguard, many publishers retain sub-editors to ensure that final copy is prepared to style before typesetting.

1.2.2 SUBMISSION ON DISK OR AS AN E-MAIL ATTACHMENT

Always ask your editor what file and disk formats are acceptable if this information does not appear in supplied guidelines. The editor will often express a preference for a particular word processor format (and graphics format where appropriate). Disks should be labelled with the author's name, the title of the work, and the software used. Do not assume that your disk will be returned.

It may be possible to submit copy as an e-mail attachment rather than on disk, but hard copy is usually required at final submission in each case.

1.2.3 CHECKING

The final version of copy should be carefully checked before delivery. All quotations should be checked against originals, and not merely against previous drafts of the work. Authors are responsible for the completeness and correctness of references. Editors will normally regard the revised version of an article as final and may refuse to accept substantive alterations to proofs or may make special charges for author corrections.

1.3 PREPARATION OF COPY

1.3.1 GENERAL

The initial submission of an article or monograph will usually be as hard copy only. Editors will circulate the text in this form to readers or referees. In the case of journal articles or conference papers sent anonymously to readers, the author's name will have to be omitted from all pages except the cover page (which the reader will not see). The final form of the text, after all necessary revisions, will normally be supplied on disk and as hard copy. The editors will use the hard copy to indicate minor amendments, to add instructions to the typesetter, and to assess the probable length of the work when made up into printed pages. The typesetter requires a printed version to ensure that all parts of the copy are present in the disk version and to resolve any problems that may arise when the word processor file is converted to the typesetter's system.

Authors should avoid the temptation to overdesign their final copy. The increasing capacity of word processors to manipulate multiple founts, type sizes, and page layout enables authors to prepare hard copy to a standard matching good typography, but many of these effects are incompatible with typesetters' systems, or are lost on conversion. In particular, automatic numbering and positioning of footnotes is not admissible (see 1.3.11), and emboldened or enlarged characters, special symbols, and proprietary founts should be avoided. Where authors wish to indicate the structure of an article or specific features of page layout, they should use conventional devices such as headings (see 1.3.4) or annotate the hard copy accordingly.

Hard copy should be clearly printed on one side only of good white paper of a standard size, preferably A4 or the American standard 8½-by-11-inch size. The pages should be numbered (see 1.3.8) and joined with a paper clip, not stapled. Authors should retain a copy of the submitted version, both on disk and as hard copy.

1.3.2 INSTRUCTIONS FOR THE TYPING OF COPY

1.3.2.1 GENERAL

Double-spacing (to allow for editorial corrections) and one size of a simple typeface should be used throughout. Margins of at least 2.5 cm (1 inch) should be left all round and the top quarter of the first page of the text left clear, for a sub-editor's additions. The first line of each paragraph (except the first paragraph of a chapter, section, or article) should be indented by one tab character, and the space between paragraphs should be the normal double line spacing. Do not indent text by inserting multiple spaces. Text should be left-justified.

Use a serif font such as Courier (or a serif typeface, if preparing copy on a typewriter), to avoid confusion of characters such as upper case 'I' and lower case 'l', which can look almost identical in sans serif typefaces such as Arial ('I' and 'l' respectively).

1.3.2.2 CORRECTIONS, INSERTIONS, AND COMMENTS

Authors who use a word processor should not make manual corrections to the hard copy but should submit a fully revised and unannotated version. Authors who use typewriters, or editors amending hard copy, may need to mark corrections. If brief, these should be added legibly above the line concerned. Proof-reading conventions and marginal marks should not be used since the typesetter needs to be able to read the text continuously. If a correction or addition is of considerable length, it should be printed on a separate sheet of paper and marked with the position at which it should be inserted (for example, 'Insert at A on page 5'). At the appropriate point in the main text write 'Insert copy A attached'. Pages with extensive alteration should be retyped: never use the reverse of the page, or copy may be overlooked.

Comments for the editor may be made in the margin in pencil. Special comments for the attention of the typesetter (see for example 1.3.13) should be written on the hard copy, encircled, and prefaced by the word 'PRINTER'.

1.3.3 FOUNTS AND CAPITALS

The typesetter will normally have available typefaces in both upper case (large capitals) and lower case, each in roman, italic, and bold versions; in addition, the system should include a typographically separate small capital fount. This should not be confused with capital letters printed in a smaller type size since small capital founts have been separately designed. These alphabets may be seen thus:

LARGE CAPITALS   SMALL CAPITALS   lower case

ITALIC CAPITALS   *italic lower case*

BOLD CAPITALS   **bold lower case**

LARGE CAPITALS should be typed as such; text to be set in SMALL CAPITALS should be typed either as such, by using the word processor's small capitals fount, or in lower case with double underlining inserted manually on the hard copy, e.g. <u>small capitals</u> (do not use the word processor's double-underline facility).

For text to be set in italic type, authors should use the word processor's italic form of a fount, which can be automatically converted, rather than typing the copy in roman type and underlining it, as is the practice when using a typewriter.

The bold form of a fount should not be used by authors (where necessary, it will be introduced by the editor). Ensure that a legible size of fount is used so that superior and inferior figures and diacritical and punctuation marks can be clearly seen.

1.3.4 HEADINGS AND SUBDIVISIONS

Do not type headings or subheadings in capitals and do not underline or italicize them, since either method may conflict with the style which the editor wishes the printer to follow. No punctuation marks (other than question marks) should be used after headings or subheadings.

Major subdivisions within the text, if required, should be marked by increased spacing. The first line of a new subdivision should not be indented. A convenient system for designating numbered subdivisions is to number all sections and subsections with arabic numerals and express them in series, divided by full points, as in this *Style Guide*.

1.3.5 DASHES

Although word processors will often have the facility to indicate a short dash or en rule (–) and a long dash or em rule (—), the following practice is recommended:

- An en rule should be represented by a hyphen with no space either side:

    The 1939-1945 war

(this will be marked up appropriately by the editor).

- An em rule should be represented by two hyphens with a space on either side:

    Some people -- an ever increasing number -- deplore this

- A 2-em rule should be represented by three hyphens together:

Marlowe, Christopher, *Edward II*
--- *The Jew of Malta*

For discussion of usage, see 4.2.

1.3.6   QUOTATION MARKS

Many word processors will automatically convert straight single and double quotation marks to 'smart quotes' (' ' and " "), and this function should be used when preparing copy for the printer. If this feature is not available, type a backward-slanting mark (`) to open single quotes and a vertical mark (') to close single quotes. For double quotation marks, type these single quotation marks twice.

1.3.7   RUNNING HEADS

Shortened headings may be required at the heads of printed pages after the first page of the article or chapter. A suitably abbreviated version of the title should be provided by the author on submission of copy and indicated at the top of the first page of the hard copy.

1.3.8   NUMBERING OF PAGES

Ensure that all pages of the hard copy (including notes or references) are numbered consecutively in the top right-hand corner, and indicate the total number of pages on the first page. If any pages are added or removed during revision the entire printed copy must be renumbered.

1.3.9   TYPING CONVENTIONS

The basic formatting of the text, particularly the division into pages and lines, should be left to the typesetter. In particular, do not use any of the ad hoc formatting devices available on your word processor, such as manual page breaks and variations of page dimensions, to fit text neatly on to whole pages. This may detract from the visual aspect of your final copy, but it will avoid any need for the typesetter to change the format of your copy before it can be processed. Use hyphens only as recommended in 2.3; do not use automatic hyphenation. The return key (or paragraph marker) should only be used at the end of paragraphs and headings, or to divide the lines of tables, lists, or verse quotations.

Double spaces should not be used in normal text, and should be eliminated from your copy before submission. In particular, type only a single space between the end of a sentence and the first character of the next, and following major punctuation marks such as colons and semicolons.

Do not right-justify or centre any parts of the text, as this introduces additional spaces which are not easily distinguished from typed spaces.

1.3.10 SPECIAL CHARACTERS AND DIACRITICS, AND NON-LATIN SCRIPTS

If your text contains unusual foreign-language characters, phonetic symbols, or other special characters or diacritics, you should consult the editor or publisher as to the best way to insert them in your copy. The special character sets provided by major word processors such as Microsoft Word are acceptable to many publishers; devices for creating and combining characters, such as provided by WordPerfect, should be avoided. When your text contains special characters or diacritics identified as problematic, highlight the first instance on the hard copy, and indicate in the margin the word processor character or string of characters used to obtain them. Some publishers specify codes for nonstandard characters; an extensive list of such codes is available to contributors to *The Year's Work in Modern Language Studies* and other MHRA publications. In extreme cases, special characters may be indicated by hand on the hard copy, or represented by specially devised codes, with appropriate indications in the margin. Where your text contains a significant number of special characters, it is advisable to list them all on a separate sheet of paper, for submission along with the final copy.

Alphabets such as Cyrillic and Greek may cause conversion problems for typesetters, who can suggest a specific method of producing the copy. For transliteration of Cyrillic characters, see 2.8. Additional problems arise with other alphabetic scripts (such as Arabic and Hebrew) and non-alphabetic scripts (such as Chinese and Japanese). In all such cases, consult the editor at an early stage.

The following publications contain much useful information on copy preparation and typesetting for languages other than English, both those using the Latin alphabet and others:

R. M. Ritter, *The Oxford Guide to Style* (Oxford: Oxford University Press, 2002), pp. 235–369

The Chicago Manual of Style, 14th edn (Chicago: University of Chicago Press, 1993), pp. 317–53

1.3.11 NOTES

Whether they are to be reproduced as footnotes or grouped together at the end of an article or chapter as endnotes, notes should be typed with double spacing and should begin on a new page of the printed version after the main text. They should be numbered consecutively throughout an article or chapter, but not throughout a whole book, and each section should be headed 'Notes to Chapter [. . .]'. The notes will normally be set in type smaller than that used for the text; they are typeset separately and the two files merged when each page is composed. Reference numbers should be typed as superior (superscript) figures, following any punctuation, and at the end of a sentence if possible:

> [. . .] composed.[23]

Do not use the standard footnoting or endnoting facility of a word processor, as the final copy would then have to be reformatted so as to make it conform to the principles laid down in the preceding paragraph.

1.3.12 ILLUSTRATIONS

For line illustrations, provide a clear original in black ink on white paper or board; for halftone illustrations, provide a glossy black-and-white photograph. Indicate clearly on the reverse of each drawing or photograph the title of the book or journal, the author's name, the figure or plate number, and the size at which the illustration is to appear. Be careful to write very lightly on the reverse of photographs or they may be spoiled. Some reduction may improve definition, but excessive reduction may cause detail, such as fine lines or close shading, to be lost. Normally the original ought not to be more than four times larger, nor should it be smaller, than the required image. A decision concerning the size of the illustration should take account of the area occupied by the type on the page of the relevant journal or book, or any other grid into which illustrations are required to fit. If part of the illustration is to be omitted, indicate lightly on the reverse or on an attached paper overlay the portion which is to be masked off. Alternatively, the area to be masked off can be indicated on a good, full-size, photocopy of the illustration.

If you wish to submit digital images, consult the editor as to the required format and means of submission.

Indicate the intended position in the text for each illustration, by insertion of the phrase 'Figure [. . .]' and, in the margin, add the note 'Figure [. . .] here'. Bear in mind that, for technical reasons, it may not be possible to place the illustration exactly where you would wish.

The term 'plate' is applicable only to pages of illustrations printed, and numbered, separately from the text, and it refers to the page, not to the illustrations on it (so one plate may contain more than one illustration). Authors who are not sure of the intended treatment of their halftone illustrations should consult the editor before numbering them.

Captions for illustrations should be typed on a separate sheet and attached to the hard copy. Illustrations should be numbered in sequence throughout an article or book, plates in roman numerals, figures in arabic. Where appropriate, the scale of an illustration in relation to the original should be indicated. Acknowledgement of permission to reproduce the illustration, where appropriate, should be indicated below the caption.

Original illustrations should be very carefully packed to avoid damage: a strong piece of cardboard in the envelope is advisable. Do not use paperclips to hold photographs together.

1.3.13 Tables

Tables may not always convert satisfactorily from word-processed files. They should be prepared using the word processor's standard table routine if possible, but, if not, columns should be separated by standard tabulation. In the hard copy tables should be printed on separate pages and their intended position in the text marked by insertion of the phrase 'Table [. . .] here' in the margin in pencil.

1.3.14 Cross-references

Since they cannot be finalized until the text is typeset, cross-references within an article or book should be typed as zeros on the hard copy and encircled in ink:

See above [or below], p.⓪⓪⓪, n. ⓪.

The page number in the hard copy referred to should be noted in pencil in the margin and such cross-references should be carefully checked and marked on the proofs.

1.3.15 Copy Produced on a Typewriter

Whilst many electric or electronic typewriters can produce effects such as underlining, it is difficult to produce the same layout as on a word processor.

For text to be set in a particular fount it should be marked (manually if necessary) as follows:

- Italic text to be underlined once
- Small capitals to be underlined twice
- Capitals to be typed in capitals, or typed in lower case and underlined three times
- Italic capitals to be typed as capitals and underlined once.

See Chapter 14, 'Proof Correction', for an illustration of these conventions.

1.4 AUTHOR-TYPESET FORMATS

1.4.1 General

Where economy or speed is an important concern, an author may be asked to prepare typeset pages in the final form in which they are to be published. This may apply to entire monographs or to items in newsletters or collections or preprints of conference papers. The author should be guided by the instructions of the volume or series editor on issues of style, usage, and formatting, to ensure consistency within the volume and between volumes. For MHRA volumes prepared by this means, authors should follow this *Style Guide*.

1.4.2   Camera-ready Copy

1.4.2.1   general

Camera-ready copy (CRC) is a printed copy of the text on single pages that is used for the production of film and printing plates without further intervention by editor or printer. This can be prepared on a word processor, using a printer's guidelines (see 1.4.2.2).

1.4.2.2   typographic style

Guidance should be sought from the printer before preparing CRC. Commonly, CRC is prepared using a page size larger than the final printed size, so that the copy can be reduced and the density of the type increased. Consistent guidelines should be drawn up, especially if a volume prepared in this way is to form one of a series. These may include a grid specifying the width and depth of the text area; the position of running heads and folios relative to the text and their location on an A4 page; a specified typeface; type sizes for text, quotations, notes, etc., capable of reduction in scale without loss of legibility; style of chapter titles and headings; and rules on word breaks and line and page ends.

1.4.2.3   presentation of crc

Camera-ready copy should be printed on high-quality white paper, using a laser printer, and to the highest resolution in terms of dots-per-inch (DPI) possible. All parts of the work should be presented in the correct order (see 1.5 below), each page being printed on one side only.

1.4.3   Direct Electronic Submission

Sophisticated word-processing and desktop publishing (DTP) software allows authors to submit their content digitally as made-up pages. This may take the form of files in the format of the program used, or PostScript or PDF files, which are used by the printer to produce printing plates. As always, it is essential to consult the printer about file formats and methods of transferring files before beginning work, and authors should still have regard to matters of style and layout as mentioned in 1.4.2.2.

1.5   ORDER OF PARTS OF A BOOK

Before submission to editor or publisher, the text of a book should be arranged in the order listed below. Authors undertaking the typesetting of a book, whether as CRC or by DTP, should have regard to this list, and to which pages (generally preliminaries) may be conventionally typeset in a series with standing matter or an established format.

Before despatch, the typescript of a book should be arranged in the following order (though few books will include all the items listed):

Half-title (the full title, including any subtitle, of the book, and the title of the series and the volume number in that series, if applicable; the name of the author does not normally appear); the verso of this page is usually left blank when the book is printed or may carry a frontispiece

Title page

Bibliographical details (name and address of the publisher and printer, copyright statement, International Standard Book Number (ISBN), Cataloguing-in-Publication Data, etc.); this page may be left blank by the author and the details supplied by the editor and publisher

Dedication or epigraph (the verso is left blank)

Contents list

List of illustrations (plates, figures, and maps, in that order)

Foreword (by someone other than the author)

Author's preface

Acknowledgements (if not included in the author's preface)

List of abbreviations and/or glossary if these are necessary to an understanding of the text; otherwise they may be placed towards the end of the book, before the bibliography

Introduction (unless this constitutes the first chapter of the text)

Text

Appendix or appendices

Notes and references (for the whole typescript)

Bibliography

Index or indexes

Colophon

The copyright should be indicated thus: international copyright symbol (©); name of holder of copyright; year of first publication. The name of the country where the book was printed must appear and may conveniently be combined with the publisher's imprint. The preliminary pages, comprising all items before the main text, are usually numbered in lower-case roman numerals; though these numbers are not printed on certain pages (half-title, title, etc.), they are counted in the sequence. Arabic numbering usually begins on the first page of the text. However, since the page numbers cannot be added by the printer until the page proofs are prepared, all the pages of the typescript should be numbered in one (arabic) sequence throughout (see 1.3.8).

2 SPELLING

2.1 PREFERRED SPELLINGS

British spelling should be used. For verbs ending in *-ize* or *-ise* and their derivatives, the forms in *-ize*, *-ization*, etc. (e.g. *civilize*, *civilization*) are preferred. Some words, because of their origin, must, however, have the *-ise* spelling, e.g.:

advertise	comprise	devise	franchise	revise
advise	compromise	enterprise	improvise	supervise
apprise	demise	excise	incise	surmise
chastise	despise	exercise	premise	surprise

Note that the British spelling of *analyse* and its derivatives has *s* and not *z*.

For other alternative spellings, the form given in *The Oxford Dictionary for Writers and Editors*, 2nd edn (Oxford: Oxford University Press, 2000) should in most cases be used (but for diacritics, see 2.2).

2.2 DIACRITICS

There is great inconsistency between dictionaries (and sometimes within the same dictionary) as to the use of accents and other diacritics on words borrowed from other languages.

Two cases are, however, clear:

(a) When a word or, more often, an expression is still felt to be foreign (and an objective decision is not always possible), all diacritics should be retained, e.g.:

aide-mémoire, ancien régime, à la mode, Aufklärung, la belle époque, bête noire, cause célèbre, déjà vu, éminence grise, Führer, lycée, maître d'hôtel, papier mâché, pièce de résistance, raison d'être, señor, succès de scandale, tête-à-tête

Such words and expressions are often italicized (see also 6.2).

(b) Words ending in *-é* retain their accent:

blasé, café, cliché, exposé, fiancé (also fiancée)

In such words, any other accents are also retained, e.g.:

émigré, pâté, protégé, résumé

We recommend that, except as provided for in (b) above, diacritics should be dropped in the case of words that have passed into regular English usage, e.g.:

chateau, creche, crepe (*but* crêpe Suzette), debacle, debris, decor, denouement, detente, echelon, elite, fete, hotel, matinee, naive, precis, premiere, regime, role, seance, soiree

For the use of accents on capitals, see 5.6.

2.3 HYPHENS

Hyphens should be used only when they have a specific purpose. They may serve to separate the parts of a complex word so as to avoid awkward sequences of letters (e.g., *re-enter*, *co-opt*) but they normally indicate that two or more words are to be read as a single word with only one main stress. The examples given below show forms that are attributive and have a single main stress and are therefore hyphenated, while predicative and other forms having two main stresses are not hyphenated:

a well-known fact	the facts are well known
a tenth-century manuscript	in the tenth century
a late-eighteenth-century novelist	written in the late eighteenth century

In phrases such as *pre- and post-war governments*, *pro- and anti-abortion movements*, *eighteenth- and nineteenth-century literature*, where two or more parallel hyphenated terms are combined, a hyphen is left hanging, i.e. it is followed by a space.

Adverbs ending in -*ly* are not hyphenated to a following adjective or participle:

a highly contentious argument
a recently published novel
a handsomely bound volume
a frequently occurring mistake

Collocations of certain monosyllabic adverbs (in particular *ill* but not *well* — see above) and a participle often have only one main stress and are therefore hyphenated even when used predicatively:

He is very ill-tempered.
Such a course of action would be ill-advised.

Note that, unlike the words *early*, *late*, *north*, *south*, etc., the prefix *mid-* always requires a hyphen (except where it forms part of a single word, as in *midnight*):

The boat sank in mid-Atlantic
a mid-June midnight flight
a mid-sixteenth-century chair
until the mid-nineteenth century

The presence or absence of a hyphen is often significant:

two-year-old dogs	two year-old dogs
a deep-blue lake	a deep blue lake
a vice-chancellor	the vice squad
to re-cover	to recover

Usage shifts over time and forms that were once entirely acceptable may now seem odd or old-fashioned. Some words that used to be hyphenated have now become so common that they are regarded as single unhyphenated words:

battlefield, bookshelf, paperback, subcommittee, subtitle

In short, if a compound is in frequent use and is pronounced as a single word it is usually acceptable to write it as one word without a hyphen. There is considerable variation in the use of hyphens and it is impossible to formulate comprehensive rules. The best advice is to use a good dictionary or spellchecker and to be consistent.

2.4 QUOTATIONS

The spelling of quotations is always that of the book or edition referred to. Note, however, that in quotations from early printed books the forms of the letters *i* and *j*, *u* and *v*, the long *s* (f), the ampersand (&), the Tironian sign (7), the tilde, superior letters in contractions, and other abbreviations are normalized to modern usage unless there are good reasons to the contrary, as, for example, in full bibliographical descriptions.

2.5 THE POSSESSIVE

The possessive of proper names ending in a pronounced -*s* or other sibilant is normally formed by adding an apostrophe and *s*:

Alvarez's criticism, Berlioz's symphonies, Cervantes's works, Dickens's characters, in Inigo Jones's day, Keats's poems, Gaston Paris's edition, Dylan Thomas's use of language

However, the possessive of *Moses* and of Greek names ending in -*es* (particularly those having more than two syllables) is frequently formed by means of an apostrophe alone:

under Moses' leadership, Demosthenes' speeches, Sophocles' plays, Xerxes' campaigns

The possessive of names ending in -*us* conforms to the normal rule:

Claudius's successor, Herodotus's *Histories*, Jesus's parables, an empire greater than Darius's

Note that French names ending in an unpronounced *-s*, *-x*, or *-z* follow the normal rule and take an apostrophe and *s*:

Rabelais's comedy, Descartes's works, Malraux's style, Cherbuliez's novels

2.6 PLACE NAMES

Where there is a current English form for foreign or other non-English place names (*Bucharest, Dunkirk, Havana, Lampeter, Lisbon, Majorca, Moscow, Munich, Naples, Quebec, Rheims, Salonika, Venice, Vienna*, etc.), it should be used. Obsolete English forms (*Carnarvon, Francfort, Leipsic*, etc.) should, however, be avoided. The forms *Luxembourg* and *Strasbourg* have now largely superseded *Luxemburg* and *Strasburg* or *Strassburg* and are therefore recommended. The English forms *Lyons* and *Marseilles* rather than the French forms (*Lyon, Marseille*) should, however, still be used in writing even though approximations to the French forms are increasingly used in pronunciation.

The use or non-use of hyphens in names such as *Newcastle upon Tyne*, *Stratford-upon-Avon* should be checked in a good reference work. Note that French place names are regularly hyphenated, e.g. *Colombey-les-Deux-Églises*, *Châlons-sur-Marne, Saint-Malo*, except for an introductory definite article, e.g. *Le Havre, Les Baux-de-Provence*.

The definite article is no longer used in the names of the countries *Lebanon, Sudan* and *Ukraine* (but *the Gambia, the Netherlands*).

For forms of reference to the place of publication of books, see 10.2.2 and 10.6.

2.7 PERSONAL NAMES

Where generally accepted English forms of classical names exist (*Horace, Livy, Ptolemy, Virgil*), they should be used.

Names of popes and saints should normally be given in their English form (*Gregory, Innocent, Paul, St Thomas Aquinas, St John of the Cross, St Francis of Assisi*).

Names of foreign kings and queens should normally be given in their English form where one exists (*Charles V, Catherine the Great, Ferdinand and Isabella, Francis I, Henry IV, Victor Emmanuel*). Those names for which no English form exists (*Haakon, Sancho*) or for which the English form is quaint or archaic (*Alphonse, Lewis* for *Alfonso, Louis*) should retain their foreign form. If in the course of a work it is necessary to refer to some monarchs whose names have acceptable English forms and some which do not, in the interests of consistency it is better to use the foreign form for all:

the reigns of Fernando III and Alfonso X
Henri IV was succeeded by Louis XIII.

2.8   SLAVONIC NAMES

Various systems exist for the transliteration of Russian and other languages using the Cyrillic alphabet. Contributors to journals, series, etc. in the field of Slavonic studies should ascertain what system is preferred and conform to it strictly. The MHRA specifies that the Library of Congress system without diacritics is to be used in all its publications in the Slavonic field, viz. *The Slavonic and East European Review*, Slavonic sections of *The Modern Language Review* and *The Year's Work in Modern Language Studies*, and relevant volumes in the Publications of the MHRA, MHRA Texts and Dissertations, and MHRA Bibliographies series.

Russian and other Slavonic names referred to in other contexts should, wherever possible, be given in the form recommended by *The Oxford Dictionary for Writers and Editors*, 2nd edn (Oxford: Oxford University Press, 2000), even when this conflicts with the Library of Congress system:

Dostoevsky, Shostakovich, Tolstoy, Yevtushenko

Note in particular that, except in the one case of *Tchaikovsky*, *Ch-* not *Tch-* should be used (e.g. *Chekhov*) and that the prime (') should not be used:

Gogol, Gorky, Ilya

(compare Library of Congress: Gogol', Gor'kii, Il'ia).

3 ABBREVIATIONS

3.1 GENERAL

Since abbreviations increase the possibility of confusion and misunderstanding, they should be used with caution. When writing for a particular publication, use only those abbreviations which are likely to be familiar to its readers. Never begin a sentence with an abbreviation, and avoid abbreviations as far as possible in passages of continuous prose. For example:

The author's comments on page 47, line 20, seem particularly apt.

Here the words 'page' and 'line', normally abbreviated in references, are given in full to prevent a disruptive effect in reading. Extensively used abbreviations, other than common ones like 'p.' and 'l.', should be clearly listed at the beginning of a book or in an early note to an article; the first use of an abbreviation should refer the reader to this list.

3.2 TITLES

Avoid inelegant or confusing abbreviations of the titles of literary works, especially in the text of your book or article. It is clearly necessary to avoid frequent repetition of a title, especially a long one, and discreet abbreviation will from time to time be needed. This should normally take the form of a short title, not initials: *All's Well*, not *AWEW*. Repetition can often be avoided in other ways: 'the play', when it is obvious which play is meant. In notes, and in parenthetical textual references in the main body of a book or article, abbreviations are more often appropriate, but they need not be inelegant and must never confuse. Note, however, that abbreviated titles are standard in some cultures, e.g. *PMC* for *Poema de mio Cid*. See 9.2 on the avoidance of repeated footnote references to the same work.

3.3 IN FOOTNOTES AND ENDNOTES

If possible, do not begin a note with an abbreviation which is normally printed in lower-case characters ('e.g.', 'i.e.', 'pp.'). If this cannot be avoided, the initial letters of footnotes should remain in lower case:

[21] pp. 127–39   *not*   [21] Pp. 127–39

3.4   USE OF FULL POINT

A contracted form of a word that ends with the same letter as the full form, including plural -*s*, is not followed by a full point:

> Mr, Dr, Mrs, Mme, Jr, St, vols

but note the exception 'no.' (for Italian 'numero'). Other abbreviations take the full point:

> M. (Monsieur), Prof., p., pp., sc., viz., vol.

In lower-case abbreviations for expressions consisting of more than one word, there is a full point after each initial:

> a.m. (*ante meridiem*), e.g. (*exempli gratia*), i.e. (*id est*), n.p. (no place [of publication]), s.h.v. (*sub hoc verbo*)

Full points are omitted in capitalized abbreviations for:

> (a) standard works of reference (italicized), journals (italicized), or series (not italicized):

> *DNB*, *OED*, *MLR*, *PMLA*, *TLS*, ANTS, EETS

> (b) countries, institutions, and organizations (none of them italicized):

> UK, USA, BL, BM, PRO, UNAM, CNRS, MHRA, MLA, UNESCO

> (c) in bibliographical references, MS, MSS ('manuscript(s)') (in normal prose text the word should be written out in full).

3.5   TRUNCATIONS

Some words are abbreviated by omitting the first part of the word. If such abbreviations are in common use, no apostrophe is needed:

> bus not 'bus
> phone not 'phone
> the twenties (i.e. 1920s) not 'twenties

3.6   AMERICAN STATES

With a few exceptions, in particular 'Cal.' and 'Mass.' which are still widely used, the official abbreviations for American states have been replaced in general use by the two-letter postal abbreviations:

> CA (California), IL (Illinois), MA (Massachusetts), NY (New York)

The postal abbreviations, which have no full point, should be used whenever it is necessary to include the name of the state in bibliographical references. These abbreviations are given in *The Oxford Dictionary for Writers and Editors*, 2nd edn (Oxford: Oxford University Press, 2000).

4 PUNCTUATION

4.1 COMMAS

In enumeration of three or more items, the words 'and' and 'or' should be preceded by a comma to avoid the possibility of ambiguity:

> The University has departments of French, German, Spanish, and Portuguese
> *but:* The University has departments of French, Spanish and Portuguese, and German.
>
> You may travel by car, bus, or train
> *but:* You may travel by car, bus or train, or bicycle.

4.2 DASHES

Printers use both a short and a long dash.

The short dash ('en rule') is used to indicate a span or a differentiation and may be considered as a substitute for 'and' or 'to' (but see 7.1):

> the England–France match; the 1939–45 war; pp. 81–101

Long dashes ('em rules') are normally found in pairs to enclose parenthetical statements, or singly to denote a break in the sentence:

> Some people — an ever increasing number — deplore this.
> Family and fortune, health and happiness — all were gone.

Long dashes should be used sparingly; commas, colons, or parentheses are often more appropriate. Other punctuation marks should not normally be used before or after a dash.

A very long dash (——), known as a '2-em dash', is used to indicate 'ditto' in bibliographies and similar lists.

For means of representing the different dashes in typescript, see 1.3.5.

4.3 PARENTHESES AND BRACKETS

In its strict sense, the term 'brackets' means 'square brackets', i.e. [ ], and should not be used with reference to parentheses, i.e. ( ). However, since it is widely misused, it is as well always to specify 'square brackets', 'round brackets' (or 'parentheses'), 'angle brackets', i.e. < >, or 'braces', i.e. { }, and avoid the use of the term 'brackets' alone.

Parentheses are used for parenthetical statements and references within a text. When a passage within parentheses falls at the end of a sentence of which it is only a part, the final full point is placed outside the closing parenthesis:

This was well reviewed at the time (for instance in *TLS*, 9 July 1971, p. 817).

When a complete sentence is within parentheses, the final full point should be inside the closing parenthesis. Parentheses may be used within parentheses:

(His presidential address (1967) made this point clearly.)

Square brackets should be used for the enclosure of phrases or words which have been added to the original text or for editorial and similar comments:

He adds that 'the lady [Mrs Jervis] had suffered great misfortunes'.
I do not think they should have [two words illegible].
He swore to tell the truth, the old [*sic*] truth, and nothing but the truth.

For the use of brackets around ellipses, see 4.8. For the use of brackets in references to the publication of books, see 10.2.2.

4.4 PUNCTUATION IN HEADINGS

Punctuation marks (other than question marks) should be omitted at the end of headings and subheadings. Punctuation marks should also be omitted after items in lists which are in tabular form (except, of course, full points used to mark abbreviations).

4.5 PUNCTUATION WITH ITALICS

There are italic forms of most punctuation marks. The type style (roman or italics) of the main part of any sentence will govern the style of the punctuation marks within or concluding it. If the main part of a sentence is in roman but an italic word within it immediately precedes a punctuation mark, that mark will normally be in roman. But if the punctuation mark occurs within a phrase or title which is entirely in italics, or if the punctuation mark belongs to the phrase in italics rather than to the sentence as a whole, the punctuation mark will be in italics:

Where is a storm more brilliantly portrayed than in Conrad's *Typhoon*?

In *Edmund Ironside; or, War Hath Made All Friends*, a play that survives in manuscript, we see this technique in operation.

Kingsley followed this with *Westward Ho!*, perhaps his best-known novel.

Who wrote *Who's Afraid of Virginia Woolf?*?

Do not follow the practice of substituting roman for italics in titles within italicized titles (e.g. *Understanding* Les Fleurs du mal: *Critical Readings*); in such cases, quotation marks should be used even if they do not figure in the original, e.g. *Understanding 'Les Fleurs du mal': Critical Readings*.

4.6   QUOTATION MARKS

See Chapter 8. For the use of quotation marks with the titles of poems, essays, etc., see 6.3.

4.7   EXCLAMATION MARKS

These should generally be avoided in scholarly writing.

4.8   ELLIPSES

In quotations, points indicating an ellipsis (i.e. the omission of a portion of the text) should be enclosed within square brackets:

> Her enquiries [. . .] were not very favourably answered.

The original punctuation is retained when it is possible to do so:

> When, in the course of human events, it becomes necessary for one people to dissolve the political bands which have connected them with another [. . .], a decent respect to the opinions of mankind requires that they should declare the causes which impel them to the separation.

> Outside the hut I stood bemused. [. . .] It was still morning and the smoke from the cookhouse rose straight to the leaden sky.

When the beginning of a sentence is omitted, the first word following the ellipsis is capitalized even if it does not have a capital in the original:

> A bugle sounded in the palace yard. [. . .] A man in the square started to sing the national anthem.

(In the original text of this last example, the second sentence reads: 'As though it were a call to arms, a man in the square started to sing the national anthem.') See also 8.6.

Following this practice makes it possible to distinguish between points indicating an ellipsis and points that occur in the original, as in the following quotation from Samuel Beckett:

> Will you never have done . . . revolving it all?

5 CAPITALS

5.1 GENERAL

Initial capitals should be used with restraint. In particular, adjectives deriving from nouns taking initial capitals are in many cases not capitalized (but see 5.3):

Alps, alpine; Bible, biblical; Satan, satanic (but Satanic with reference to Satan himself)

Capitals must, however, be used for the initial letters of sentences and for the names of places, persons, nationalities, the days of the week, and months (but not for the seasons of the year). They are also to be used for the titles of laws, plans, wars, treaties, legal cases, and for specific institutions and other organizations (the Modern Humanities Research Association, the Poetry Book Club). Capitals are used also for unique events and periods (the Flood, the Iron Age, the Peasants' Revolt, the Reformation, the Enlightenment, the French Revolution, World War II, the Last Judgement) and for parts of books when referred to specifically (Chapter 9, Appendix A, Figure 8, Part 11). Names of the points of the compass are capitalized only when abbreviated (N.) or when they indicate a specific area (the North [of England], South America) or a political concept (the West). The corresponding adjectives are capitalized when they are part of an official name (Northern Ireland) or when they refer to political concepts rather than merely to geographical areas (Western Europe) but not otherwise (northern England). 'Middle' is capitalized in such fixed expressions as Middle East(ern), Middle Ages, Middle English.

Dictionaries are often inconsistent in their use or non-use of capitals for adjectives, verbs, and nouns deriving from names of peoples or languages. We recommend that capitals be used in such cases:

Americanize, Anglicization, Gallicism, Latinate

Note, however, that 'anglophone', 'francophone', etc., 'arabic numerals' and 'roman type' are not capitalized (but 'the Arabic language', 'the Roman alphabet').

5.2 TITLES AND DIGNITIES

Capitals are used for titles and dignities when these appear in full or immediately preceding a personal name, or when they are used specifically, but not otherwise:

The Archbishop of Canterbury and several other bishops were present, but Bishop Wilberforce was not.

When, after a first full reference, or with such reference understood, a title is used incompletely but still with specific application to an individual, the capital is retained:

The Archbishop spoke first.

A word or phrase used as a substitute for, or an extension of, a personal name also takes initial capitals:

the Iron Duke, Alfred the Great, the Dark Lady of the Sonnets

5.3   MOVEMENTS AND PERIODS

Capitals must be used for nouns and adjectives denoting cultural, philosophical, literary, critical, and artistic movements and periods when these are derived from proper nouns:

Cartesian, Chomskyan, Christian, Erastian, Freudian, Platonism

They should also be used for literary and other movements when the use of a lower-case initial might cause confusion with the same word in a more general sense:

a poet of the Romantic school
a novel with a straightforwardly romantic plot

This covers the use of capitals when terms such as Conservative, Democrat(ic), Independent, Liberal, National(ist), Republican, Social(ist) refer to specific political parties or movements, e.g. the Independent Labour Party, the Social and Liberal Democrats, but not otherwise, e.g. 'a man of conservative (*or* liberal) views'.

For movements and periods with the prefix 'neo', see 5.5.2.

5.4   TITLES OF BOOKS AND OTHER WRITINGS

In most modern European languages except English and French, and in Latin and transliterated Slavonic languages, capitalization in the titles of books, series, articles, essays, poems, etc. follows the rules of capitalization in normal prose. That is, the first word and all proper nouns (in German all nouns) take an initial capital, and all other words take a lower-case initial:

La vida es sueño; El alcalde de Zalamea; Il seme sotto la neve; De senectute; Autorenlexikon der deutschen Gegenwartsliteratur; Obras clássicas da literatura portuguesa

In English titles the initial letters of the first word and of all nouns, pronouns (except the relative 'that'), adjectives, verbs, adverbs, and subordinating conjunctions are capitalized, but those of articles, possessive determiners ('my', etc.), prepositions, and the co-ordinating conjunctions 'and', 'but', 'or', and 'nor' are not:

> (books) *Put Out More Flags*; *How Far Can You Go?*; *The Man Who Was Thursday*; *All's Well that Ends Well*; *Pride and Prejudice*, *A Voyage towards the South Pole*; (series) A Social History of the Welsh Language; (poems) 'The Passionate Shepherd to his Love'

The first word of a subtitle following a colon is capitalized:

> *Strange Music: The Metre of the English Heroic Line*
> *The Wild Card of Reading: On Paul de Man*

but '*or*', introducing an alternative title after a semi-colon, is not:

> *All for Love; or, The World Well Lost*

English works with foreign titles are normally capitalized according to the English convention rather than that of the language of the title:

> *Religio Medici*; 'Portrait d'une Femme'; 'La Figlia che Piange'

In French titles it is normally only the initial letters of the first word and of proper nouns which are capitalized. But if the first word is a definite article, the following noun and any preceding adjectives also take an initial capital:

> *Le Médecin malgré lui*; *Les Grands Cimetières sous la lune*; *Un début dans la vie*; *Une ténébreuse affaire*; *Du latin aux langues romanes*; *Nouveau cours de grammaire*; *Histoire de la littérature française*; *A la recherche du temps perdu*

However, for reasons of symmetry, capitals are sometimes used elsewhere:

> 'Le Corbeau et le Renard'; *Le Rouge et le Noir*

Capitalization in the titles of journals is inconsistent. In particular, in French titles initials of some or all nouns and adjectives are sometimes capitalized, e.g. *Revue de Linguistique Romane*. We recommend that one or other of the following procedures be adopted:

(a) follow the general rules for capitalization given above
or (b) adopt the preferred style of each journal.

In either case, be consistent throughout a given piece of work.

5.5   HYPHENATED COMPOUNDS

5.5.1   TITLES AND HEADINGS

In titles and headings, capitalize the first part of the compound and capitalize the second part if it is a noun, or an adjective derived from a proper noun, or if it is equal in importance to the first part:

> Non-Christian, Anglo-Jewish Literature, Seventeenth-Century Music, Vice-Chairman

The second part does not take a capital if it merely modifies the first part or if both parts are essentially one word:

> Democracy Re-established

5.5.2   IN THE BODY OF THE TEXT

Except in titles and headings, words that would normally be capitalized retain their capital after a hyphenated prefix:

> anti-Semitism, non-Christian, post-Darwinian, pre-Columbian

In denoting cultural, philosophical, literary, critical, and artistic movements and periods, the prefix 'neo' should not be capitalized. If the earlier movement or period to which the prefix is attached does not take an initial capital, then the compound should be written as one word:

> neoclassical, neoscholastic, neocolonialism

If the original movement or period is normally capitalized (see 5.3), the compound should be hyphenated:

> neo-Aristotelianism, neo-Platonic, neo-Cartesian

It should be noted, however, that archaeologists and historians, when referring to prehistoric eras, tend to write them as one word, capitalized when a noun but not when an adjective:

> before the Neolithic, neolithic sites

5.6   ACCENTED CAPITALS

Accents should be retained on all capitals in foreign languages if they would be used on the equivalent lower-case letters. The single exception to this is the French word *à*, which drops the accent when capitalized (*A bientôt!* 'See you soon!').

5.7 SMALL CAPITALS

Small capitals are specially designed capitals, the height and visual weight of which approximate to those of lower-case letters. They are normally used for roman volume numbers, postal codes, professional and academic qualifications, and 'AD' and 'BC'. They also provide an alternative to italic and bold type in the typographic treatment of subheadings. For further guidance on roman numerals, see 7.3.

For the presentation of small capitals when preparing copy, see 1.3.3 and 1.3.15.

6 ITALICS

6.1 GENERAL

Avoid the use of italics for rhetorical emphasis. Any word or phrase individually discussed should, however, be in italics, and any interpretation of it in single quotation marks:

> He glosses *pale* as 'fenced land, park'.

It may also be desirable to use italics to distinguish one word or phrase from another, as, for example, in 7.1.

If you are in doubt about whether to italicize a word, type it as though it were not italic and draw the editor's attention to it in a marginal note. It is easier for an editor to mark a roman word for italic setting than to delete an underline or to mark italic typing for roman setting.

6.2 FOREIGN WORDS AND QUOTATIONS

Single words or short phrases in foreign languages not used as direct quotations should be in italics. Direct, acknowledged, or more substantial quotations should be in roman type (in small print or within single quotation marks). For the setting of quotations, see Chapter 8.

Foreign words and phrases which have passed into regular English usage should not be italicized, though the decision between italic and roman type may sometimes be a fine one. In doubtful instances it is usually best to use roman. The following are examples of words which are no longer italicized:

avant-garde	dilettante	milieu	role
cliché	ennui	par excellence	salon
debris	genre	per cent	status quo
denouement	leitmotif	résumé	vice versa

See also 2.2 and *The Oxford Dictionary for Writers and Editors*, 2nd edn (Oxford: Oxford University Press, 2000).

Certain Latin words and abbreviations which are in common English usage are also no longer italicized. For example:

> cf., e.g., et al., etc., ibid., i.e., passim, viz.

Exceptions are made of the Latin *sic*, frequently used within quotations (see 4.3) and therefore conveniently differentiated by the use of italic, and of *circa* (abbreviated as *c.*, see 7.1). See also 10.3 on the use of such abbreviations.

6.3   TITLES OF BOOKS AND OTHER WRITINGS

Italics are used for the titles of all works individually published under their own titles: books, journals, plays, longer poems, pamphlets, and any other entire published works. However, titles such as 'the Bible', 'the Koran', and 'the Talmud' are printed in roman, as are titles of books of the Bible (see 10.2.8). Titles of series are not italicized, e.g. 'Theory and History of Literature'. The titles of chapters in books or of articles in books or journals should be in roman type enclosed within single quotation marks (see 10.2.3 and 10.2.4). The titles of poems, short stories, or essays which form part of a larger volume or other whole, or the first lines of poems used as titles, should also be given in roman type in single quotation marks:

> Théophile Gautier's 'L'Art'; Keats's 'Ode on a Grecian Urn'; Shelley's 'Music, When Soft Voices Die'; Joyce's 'The Dead'; Bacon's 'Of Superstition'

The titles of collections of manuscripts should be given in roman type without quotation marks (see 10.2.9). The titles of unpublished theses should be given in roman type in single quotation marks (see 10.2.6).

Titles of other works which appear within an italicized title should be printed in italics and enclosed within single quotation marks:

> *An Approach to 'Hamlet'*

In the citation of legal cases the names of the contending parties are given in italics, but the intervening 'v.' (for 'versus') is in roman:

> *Bardell* v. *Pickwick*

6.4   TITLES OF FILMS, MUSICAL COMPOSITIONS, AND WORKS OF ART

Titles of films, substantial musical compositions, and works of art are italicized:

> *The Great Dictator*; *Il Trovatore*; *Elijah*; *Swan Lake*; Beethoven's *Eroica Symphony*; *Tapiola*; *Die schöne Müllerin*; *Goyescas*; *The Haywain*; *The Laughing Cavalier*; Epstein's *Christ in Majesty*

Descriptive or numerical titles such as the following, however, take neither italics nor quotation marks:

> Beethoven's Third Symphony; Bach's Mass in B minor; Mendelssohn's Andante and Scherzo; Piano Concerto No. 1 in B flat minor

Titles of songs and other short individual pieces (like those of poems; see 6.3) are given in roman and within single quotation marks:

> 'Who is Sylvia?'; 'La Marseillaise'; 'Mercury, the Winged Messenger' from Holst's *The Planets*

7 DATES, NUMBERS, CURRENCY, AND WEIGHTS AND MEASURES

7.1 DATES

Dates should be given in the form '23 April 1564'. The name of the month should always appear in full between the day ('23' *not* '23rd') and the year. No internal punctuation should be used except when a day of the week is mentioned, e.g. 'Friday, 12 October 2001'. If it is necessary to refer to a date in both Old and New Styles, the form '11/21 July 1605' should be used. For dates dependent upon the time of beginning the new year the form '21 January 1564/5' should be used. When referring to a period of time use the form 'from 1826 to 1850' (*not* 'from 1826–50'), 'from January to March 1970' (*not* 'from January–March 1970'). In citations of the era, 'BC', 'BCE', and 'CE' follow the year and 'AD' precedes it, and small capitals without full points are used:

> 54 BC, 54 BCE, 367 CE, AD 367

With reference to centuries, all of these, including 'AD', follow:

> in the third century AD

In references to decades, an *s* without an apostrophe should be used:

> the 1920s (*not* the 1920's)

In references to centuries the ordinal should be spelled out:

> the sixteenth century (*not* the 16th century)
> sixteenth-century drama

In giving approximate dates *circa* should be abbreviated as *c.*:

> *c.* 1490, *c.* 300 BC

7.2 NUMBERS

Numbers up to one hundred, including ordinals, should be written in words when the context is not statistical. Figures should be used for volume, part, chapter, and page numbers; but note:

> The second chapter is longer than the first.

Figures are also used for years, including those below one hundred (see 7.1). But numbers at the beginning of sentences and approximate numbers should be expressed in words, as should 'hundred', 'thousand', 'million', 'billion', etc., if they appear as whole numbers:

Two hundred and forty-seven pages were written.
The fire destroyed about five thousand books.
She lived and wrote a thousand years ago.

Words should be preferred to figures where inelegance would otherwise result:

He asked for ninety soldiers and received nine hundred and ninety.

In expressing inclusive numbers falling within the same hundred, the last two figures should be given:

13–15, 44–47, 100–22, 104–08, 1933–39

Dates before the Christian era should be stated in full since the shorter form could be misleading:

Nebuchadnezzar (1792–1750 BC) (*not* (1792–50 BC))

Numbers up to 9999 are written without a comma, e.g. 2589; those from 10,000 upwards take a comma, e.g. 125,397; those with seven or more digits take two or more commas, separating groups of three digits counting from the right, e.g. 9,999,000,000. However, where digits align in columns, in copy such as tables or accounts, commas must be consistently included or omitted in all numbers above 999.

7.3 ROMAN NUMERALS

The use of roman numerals should be confined to a few specific purposes:

(a) large capitals for the ordinals of monarchs, popes, etc. (Edward VII), and for major subdivisions within a text;

(b) small capitals for volume numbers of books (journals and series take arabic numerals), also for the acts of plays, for 'books' or other major subdivisions of long poems, novels, etc., and for certain documents (see 10.2.7);

(c) small capitals for centuries in some languages other than English (xvie siècle, siglo xvii); however, in Cyrillic script large capitals are used;

(d) lower case for the preliminary pages of a book or journal, where these are numbered separately, and for minor subdivisions within a text; inclusive numbers are written out in full, e.g. 'xxiv–xxviii' not 'xxiv–viii'.

7.4 CURRENCY

Words should be used to express simple sums of money occurring in normal prose:

The manuscript was sold for eight shillings in 1865.
The reprint costs twenty-five pounds.
The fee was three hundred francs.

Names of foreign currencies should be given in their English form where one is in common use, e.g. 'mark' or 'deutschmark' (*not* 'deutsche Mark'), '[Swedish] crown', etc. Note too the use of English plurals such as 'drachmas, pfennigs' (*but* '[Italian] lire').

Sums of money which are awkward to express in words, or sums occurring in statistical tables, etc., may be written in figures. British currency before 1971 should be shown in the following form:

The manuscript was sold for £197 12s. 6d. in 1965.

British decimal currency should be expressed in pounds and pence separated by a full point on the line, not by a comma:

£12.65 (*not* £12,65 or £12.65p)

Sums below one pound should be shown thus (without a full point after 'p'):

84p, 6p

The same conventions apply to sums expressed in euros, dollars, or yen:

€250, $500, $8.95, 25c, ¥2000

Where it is necessary to specify that reference is to the American, Canadian, or some other dollar, an appropriate abbreviation precedes the symbol without a full point or a space:

US$, C$ (*or* Can$), A$ (*or* Aus$), NZ$

In most cases, abbreviations for (Swiss) francs, Scandinavian crowns, or pre-2002 European currencies follow the figure, from which they are separated by a space, and are not followed by a full point, e.g. '95 F, 250 Kr' (BF, FF, SwF, DKr, NKr, SKr where it is necessary to specify Belgian, French, Swiss, Danish, Norwegian, or Swedish currency). However, the abbreviation 'DM' for the German mark precedes the figure and is separated from it by a space, e.g. 'DM 8'.

The names of other currencies are best written out in full:

350 escudos, 500 pesetas, 20 roubles

7.5　WEIGHTS AND MEASURES

In non-statistical contexts express weights and measures in words:

He bought a phial of laudanum and an ounce of arsenic at a pharmacy two miles from Cheapside.

In statistical works or in subjects where frequent reference is made to them, weights and measures may be expressed in figures with appropriate abbreviations:

> The priory is situated 3 km from the village of Emshall.
> The same 13 mm capitals were used by three Madrid printers at different times.

Note that most such abbreviations do not take a full point or plural *s*:

> 1 kg, 15 kg, 1 mm, 6 cm, 15 m, 4 l (litres), 2 ft, 100 lb, 10 oz,

but, to avoid ambiguity, use 'in.' for 'inch(es)'.

8 QUOTATIONS AND QUOTATION MARKS

8.1 GENERAL

Quotation marks should normally be reserved for indicating direct quotations, definitions of words, or for similar functions. Avoid the practice of using quotation marks as an oblique excuse for a loose, slang, or imprecise (and possibly inaccurate) word or phrase.

In quoted passages follow the original for spelling, capitalization, italics, and punctuation (but see 2.4, 8.3, and 8.4).

8.2 IN LANGUAGES OTHER THAN ENGLISH

Quotations in languages other than English are treated in the same way as those in English (see 6.2). Unless there are special reasons to the contrary, the forms of quotation marks in foreign languages (« » „ " etc.) should be normalized to English usage.

8.3 SHORT QUOTATIONS

Short quotations (not more than about forty words of prose or two complete lines of verse) should be enclosed in single quotation marks and run on with the main text. If, however, there are several such short quotations coming close together and being compared or contrasted, or otherwise set out as examples, it may be appropriate to treat them in the same way as longer quotations (see 8.4). If not more than two complete lines of verse are quoted but the quotation includes a line division, this should be marked with a spaced upright stroke (|). For a quotation within a quotation, double quotation marks should be used:

> Mrs Grose replies that 'Master Miles only said "We must do nothing but what she likes!"'.

If a short quotation is used within a sentence, the final full point should be outside the closing quotation mark; it may also be appropriate to alter an initial capital in such a quotation to lower case:

> Do not be afraid of what Stevenson calls 'a little judicious levity'.

> Carton's assertion that 'it is a far, far better thing that I do, than I have ever done' has become almost proverbial.

This rule applies even when a quotation ends with a full point in the original, and when a quotation forms a complete sentence in the original but, as quoted, is integrated within a sentence of introduction or comment without intervening punctuation:

> We learn at once that 'Miss Brooke had that kind of beauty which seems to be thrown into relief by poor dress'.

For quotations which are either interrogatory or exclamatory, punctuation marks should appear both before and after the closing quotation mark:

> The pause is followed by Richard's demanding 'will no man say "Amen"?'.
>
> Why does Shakespeare give Malcolm the banal question 'Oh, by whom?'?

The final full point should precede the closing quotation mark only when the quotation forms a complete sentence and is separated from the preceding passage by a punctuation mark. Such a quotation may be interrupted:

> Wilde said, 'He found in stones the sermons he had already hidden there.'
>
> Soames added: 'Well, I hope you both enjoy yourselves.'
>
> Hardy's *Satires of Circumstance* was not well received. 'The gloom', wrote Lytton Strachey in his review of it, 'is not even relieved by a little elegance of diction.'

In this last example, the comma after 'gloom' follows the quotation mark as there is no comma in the original. Contrast:

> 'It is a far, far better thing that I do,' Carton asserts, 'than I have ever done'

in which the original has a comma after 'I do'. But when the quotation ends in a question mark or an exclamation mark, it is not followed by a comma:

> 'What think you of books?' said he.

When a short quotation is followed by a reference in parentheses, the final punctuation should follow the closing parenthesis:

> He assumes the effect to be 'quite deliberate' (p. 29).
>
> There is no reason to doubt the effect of this 'secret humiliation' (Book 6, Chapter 52).

8.4 LONG QUOTATIONS

Long quotations (more than about forty words of prose, prose quotations consisting of more than one paragraph even if less than forty words, and verse quotations of more than two lines) should be broken off by an increased space from the preceding and following lines of typescript. A long quotation should never be used in the middle of a sentence of the main text: it is unreasonable to expect the reader to carry the sense of a sentence across a quotation several lines in length.

Long quotations should not be enclosed within quotation marks. A quotation occurring within such a long quotation should be in single quotation marks; if a further quotation occurs within that, double quotation marks should be used. Foreign forms of quotation marks should not be preserved unless there are special reasons for doing so (see 8.2).

Prose quotations, including the first line, should not be indented; verse quotations should follow the lineation and indentation of the original. These longer quotations should be double spaced and they should be marked by a vertical line in the margin to indicate that they are to be printed in the form which is standard for the publication concerned. To assist the printer, a long quotation should be marked with an encircled note 'verse' or 'prose' in the margin if there is any possibility of doubt.

When printed, a long quotation may be distinguished from the main text by setting it in a smaller size, indenting it, or a combination of the two. The preparation and marking of the typescript in the manner described would, however, be suitable for any likely style of printing.

Long quotations should normally end with a full point; even though the original may use other punctuation, there is no need (except for a question mark or exclamation mark) to preserve this at the end of a quotation. The initial letter of the first word of a quotation may also be changed to or from a capital if this is more appropriate in the context (see 4.8).

Avoid interpolations indicating source that introduce square brackets into the opening lines of long quotations, e.g.:

> This play [writes Dr Johnson, referring to *Cymbeline*] has many just sentiments, some natural dialogues, and some pleasing scenes, but they are obtained at the expense of much incongruity.

The need for any such formulation can be eliminated by rephrasing, e.g.:

> Referring to *Cymbeline*, Dr Johnson writes:

> This play has many just sentiments, some natural dialogues, and some pleasing scenes.

A reference in parentheses after a long quotation should always be placed outside the closing full point, and without a full point of its own (see first example in 8.5).

8.5   QUOTATIONS FROM PLAYS

Where a quotation from a play is longer than about forty words, or two lines of verse, it should be treated as a long quotation (see 8.4). Whilst the spelling and punctuation within the text should be preserved, general rules may be applied to the treatment of speakers' names and stage directions.

Identify a long quotation by drawing a vertical line in the margin to the full depth of the quotation. 'Prose' or 'verse' should be written in the margin and encircled and, where a single quotation contains prose and blank verse, special care should be taken to indicate the point at which one ends and the other begins. Where a line of text is indented in the original, it should be typed as near as possible to its original position and the printer instructed in an encircled marginal note to 'follow typescript for indent'.

Most academic publishers have well-established conventions that should be observed when preparing a typescript. The following rules apply to MHRA publications in which quotations from plays appear.

Prose quotations are set full out with the speakers' names in small capitals, without final punctuation but followed by a space. Second and subsequent lines of a speech are indented. Stage directions within a line of text are set in italic type within roman parentheses. If a stage direction immediately follows a speaker's name, the space preceding the text is placed at the end of the stage direction, after the closing parenthesis. Stage directions which occupy a line on their own are indented further than the text, and set in italic type without parentheses. No extra space is inserted between speakers:

BRASSBOUND   It will teach other scoundrels to respect widows and orphans. Do you forget that there is such a thing as justice?

LADY CICELY (*gaily shaking out the finished coat*)   Oh, if you are going to dress yourself in ermine and call yourself Justice, I give you up. You are just your uncle over again; only he gets £5000 a year for it, and you do it for nothing.

She holds the coat up to see whether any further repairs are needed.

BRASSBOUND (*sulkily*)   You twist my words very cleverly. (*Captain Brassbound's Conversion*, II)

Verse quotations are usually centred on the text measure with the speakers' names positioned to the left of the text:

MACBETH   Prithee, peace!
                 I dare do all that may become a man;
                 Who dares do more, is none.

LADY MACBETH   What beast was't then
                 That made you break this enterprise to me?
                 When you durst do it, then you were a man;
                 And to be more than what you were, you would
                 Be so much more the man. Nor time nor place
                 Did then adhere, and yet you would make both;
                 They have made themselves, and that their fitness now
                 Does unmake you.

8.6   OMISSIONS

Omissions within prose quotations should be marked by an ellipsis (three points within square brackets; see 4.8). Omitted lines of verse should be marked by an ellipsis on a separate line:

> I am not covetous for gold,
> [. . .]
> But if it be a sin to covet honour
> I am the most offending soul alive.

It is not normally necessary to use an ellipsis at the beginning or end of a quotation; almost all quotations will be taken from a larger context and there is usually no need to indicate this obvious fact unless the sense of the passage quoted is manifestly incomplete.

8.7 COPYRIGHT

It is the responsibility of an author to obtain permission for the quotation of any copyright material if such permission is necessary. Normally it is unnecessary to seek permission for the quotation of brief passages in a scholarly work.

It is not possible to give a definitive ruling to indicate when it is necessary to seek permission: copyright laws are not the same in all countries, and publishers hold differing views on the subject.

In general it may be said that the length of the quoted passage and the use to which it is put should be fair to the author and publisher of the work quoted in that nothing is done to diminish the value of their publication.

Complete items such as tables, illustrations, and poems must not be reproduced without permission.

9 FOOTNOTES AND ENDNOTES

9.1 GENERAL

The term 'notes' as used in this chapter applies equally to footnotes and to endnotes (i.e. notes printed at the end of an article, chapter, or book).

Notes are an interruption to the reader and should be limited to what is strictly necessary. They are intended primarily for documentation and for the citation of sources relevant to the text. They should not be used to provide additional bibliographical material on the general subject being treated, but which is not directly needed. Nor should they normally include extra expository material. Such material, if apposite and useful, is often better incorporated into the text or added as an appendix. Only after the most careful consideration should it be included in a note.

All notes, whether or not they form complete sentences, should end with full points.

9.2 METHODS OF LIMITING NOTES

Simple references (such as line numbers or page references to a book already cited in full) can usually be incorporated in the text, normally in parentheses after quotations. A string of note references to the same text can be avoided by stating after the first full note citation: 'Further references [to this edition, etc.] are given after quotations in the text.' (See also 10.3.)

The number of notes can often be kept down by grouping together, in one note, references to several sources mentioned close together in the same paragraph. In particular, adjacent references to several pages of the same publication should be cited together in a single note. No note, however, should document references for more than one paragraph.

Notes should not repeat information already clear from the text: if, for example, the author has been named before a quotation there is no need to repeat the name in a note reference. If there is a bibliography to a book or article, notes can also be reduced.

9.3 POSITION AND NUMBERING

Wherever possible, a note reference number should be placed at the end of a sentence. Notes should be marked in the typescript by superior numbers, with no punctuation (full points, parentheses, etc.), in sequence throughout an article or chapter. A note reference number should follow any punctuation except a dash, which it should precede. It should appear at the end of a quotation, not following the author's name if that precedes the quotation.

A note reference number in the text should never be repeated to refer to the same note; if the same material has to be referred to again, a parenthetical reference in the text — '(see note 1 above)' — is the best method, though a new note using those words is a possible alternative.

Do not attach a note number to a heading or subheading; an asterisk may, however, be used to indicate a general note to an entire chapter. Nor should a note number (or, indeed, an asterisk) be attached to the title of an article; a note attached to the first or last sentence, or an unnumbered note preceding the numbered ones, is preferable.

10 REFERENCES

10.1 GENERAL

References (in the body of the text or in notes) should document the information offered, to allow the reader to check the source of a quotation or the evidence on which an argument is based. A reference must therefore enable the reader to find the source referred to as quickly and easily as possible.

A work of literature should be quoted or referred to in a satisfactory scholarly edition. If a literary or critical work is published both in Britain and overseas, the British edition should be used unless there are special reasons for doing otherwise. If an edition other than the first is used, this should be stated. If an unrevised reprint is used (such as a modern facsimile reprint of an out-of-print work or a paperback reissue of an earlier book), the publication details of the original edition as well as of the reprint should be given. Details of original publication should also be provided where an article from a journal is reprinted in an anthology of criticism (see 10.2.3): a reader looking for the article in a library is often more likely to find the original journal than the anthology. In referring to works of literature of which several editions may be available, it is often helpful to give the reader more information than merely the page number of the edition used:

> p. 235 (Book III, Chapter 4)

Similarly, when quoting a letter from a collection, it may be helpful to cite the date as well as the page number:

> p. 281 (23 April 1864)

Full references to well-known works (*OED*, *DNB*, etc.) are normally unnecessary, though for encyclopedias and biographical dictionaries of multiple authorship it is often relevant to name the writer of the article cited.

It is usually necessary to give full publication details only on the first occasion a book or article is referred to; thereafter it should be cited in an abbreviated form (see 10.3).

10.2 FORMS OF REFERENCE

10.2.1 GENERAL

Except when the author–date system (see 10.4) is used, the first reference to a book, article, or other publication should be given in full and later references in an easily identifiable abbreviated form (see 10.3).

10.2.2 Books

Full references should be given as in the following examples:

(a) Tom McArthur, *Worlds of Reference: Lexicography, Learning and Language from the Clay Tablet to the Computer* (Cambridge: Cambridge University Press, 1986), p. 59.

(b) Carlos Fuentes, *Aura*, ed. by Peter Standish, Durham Modern Language Series: Hispanic Texts, 1 (Durham: University of Durham, 1986), pp. 12–16 (p. 14).

(c) Jean Starobinski, *Montaigne in Motion*, trans. by Arthur Goldhammer (Chicago: University of Chicago Press, 1986), p. 174.

(d) *Emily Dickinson: Selected Letters*, ed. by Thomas H. Johnson, 2nd edn (Cambridge, MA: Harvard University Press, 1985), pp. 194–97.

(e) *Approaches to Teaching Voltaire's 'Candide'*, ed. by R. Waldinger (New York: Modern Language Association of America, 1987), p. 3.

(f) *Boswell: The English Experiment 1785–1789*, ed. by Irma S. Lustig and Frederick A. Pottle, The Yale Edition of the Private Papers of James Boswell (London: Heinemann; New York: McGraw Hill, 1986), pp. 333–37.

(g) *The Works of Thomas Nashe*, ed. by R. B. McKerrow, 2nd edn, rev. by F. P. Wilson, 5 vols (Oxford: Oxford University Press, 1958), III, 94–98 (pp. 95–96).

(h) H. Munro Chadwick and N. Kershaw Chadwick, *The Growth of Literature*, 3 vols (Cambridge: Cambridge University Press, 1932–40; repr. 1986), I, p. xiii.

(i) José Amador de los Ríos, *Historia crítica de la literatura española*, 7 vols (Madrid: the author, 1861–65; repr. Madrid: Gredos, 1969), VI (1865), 44–54.

(j) *Dictionary of the Middle Ages*, ed. by Joseph R. Strayer and others (New York: Scribner, 1982–89), VI (1985), 26.

(k) Hugo von Hofmannsthal, *Sämtliche Werke*, ed. by Rudolf Hirsch and others (Frankfurt a.M.: Fischer, 1975–), XIII: *Dramen*, ed. by Roland Haltmeier (1986), pp. 12–22.

(l) Debra Linowitz Wentz, *Fait et fiction: les formules pédagogiques des 'Contes d'une grand-mère' de George Sand* (Paris: Nizet, 1985), p. 9.

The information should be given in the following order:

1. *Author*: The author's name should be given as it appears on the title page; forenames should not be reduced to initials. The names of up to three authors should be given in full; for works by more than three authors the name of only the first should be given, followed by 'and others'. If the author's name is more conveniently included within the title (as, for example, in editions of 'Works'), or if the book is an edited collection or anthology, the title will appear first (see examples (d), (e), (f), (g)).

2. *Title*: The title should be given as it appears on the title page (although very long titles may be suitably abbreviated) and italicized. A colon should always be used to separate title and subtitle, even where the punctuation on the title page is different or (as often happens) non-existent. For books

in English, capitalize the initial letter of the first word after the colon and of all principal words throughout the title (see examples (a), (d), (f)); for titles in other languages, follow the capitalization rules for the language in question (see 5.4 and examples (i), (k), (l)). If figures occur in titles, these should also be italicized (see example (f)). Titles of other works occurring within the title should be enclosed in quotation marks (see examples (e), (l)). For books (usually older works) with alternative titles, punctuation before and after 'or' should be as follows:

> *The Queen; or, The Excellency of her Sex*
> *All for Love; or, The World Well Lost*

3. *Editor, Translator, etc.*: The names of editors, etc. should be treated in the same way as those of authors (as set out above) with regard to forenames and number to be given; they should be preceded by the accepted abbreviated forms 'ed. by', 'trans. by', 'rev. by' (see examples (b), (c), (d), (e), (f), (g), (j), (k)). For multi-volume works where there is more than one editor or group of editors involved, the information should be conveyed as in example (k); but see example (g) where only one editor is involved.

4. *Series*: If a book is part of a numbered series, the series title and the number (in arabic numerals) should be given (see example (b)). However, the name of the series may be omitted if it is unnumbered, unless the series title itself conveys important information (see example (f)). Series titles should not be italicized or put between quotation marks.

5. *Edition*: If the edition used is other than the first, this should be stated in the form '2nd edn', 'rev. edn' (see examples (d), (g)).

6. *Number of Volumes*: If the work is in more than one volume, the number of volumes should be given in the form '2 vols' (see examples (g), (h), (i)). Foreign equivalents, such as 'tome', 'Band', 'tomo', should be rendered as 'vol.' (see example (i)).

7. *Details of Publication*: The place of publication, the name of the publisher, and the date of publication should be enclosed in parentheses; a colon separates the place from the publisher, a comma separates the publisher from the date. Any detail of publication which is not given in the book itself but can be ascertained should be enclosed in square brackets, e.g. '[1987]', '[Paris]'. For details that are assumed but uncertain, use the form '[1987(?)]', '[Paris(?)]'. If any detail is unknown and cannot be ascertained, the following abbreviated forms of reference should be used: '[n.p.]' (= no place), '[n. pub.]' (= no publisher), '[n.d.]' (= no date). Do not use square brackets in a reference for any other purpose (for example, when the reference is already in parentheses), otherwise the impression may be conveyed that the information in brackets is uncertain.

In giving the place of publication, current English forms of place names should be used (e.g. Brussels, Geneva, Vienna, Milan, Munich; see 2.6).

The abbreviated forms of names of American states (see 3.6) should be included if there is danger of confusion (e.g. Cambridge, MA; Athens, GA). These may be omitted if the name of the state appears in the name of the publisher (e.g. Athens: University of Georgia Press). For books published by the same publisher in more than one place, it is normally sufficient to refer only to the first. Place of publication should be omitted only when (as, for example, in a bibliographical article) there are likely to be a great many references to books published at one place. In these circumstances, provide an early footnote in the form of 'Place of publication of all books cited is London [or Paris, etc.] unless otherwise stated'.

The name of the publisher (preceded by a colon) should be given without secondary matter such as '& Co.', 'Ltd', 'S.A.', etc. 'Press', 'Verlag', 'Editorial', etc. should be used only if the publishing house is not named after a person (with the exception of 'Clarendon Press'):

Éditions de la Femme; Harvester Press; Oxford University Press

It is not normally necessary to include forenames or initials of publishers, unless there are two or more with the same surname:

Maney (*not* W. S. Maney); Heinemann (*not* William Heinemann)

Where a publisher's name includes 'and' or '&', the conjunction should be given in the form which appears on the title page:

Thames and Hudson; Grant & Cutler

A book which has more than one place of publication and a different publisher in each place should be referred to as in example (f).

Details of facsimile reprints of old books should be given as in example (h) where the original publisher is responsible for the reprint, and as in example (i) where different publishers are involved. Example (i) also illustrates the appropriate form of reference to a work published by its author.

A reference to a work in several volumes published over a period of years but now complete should state the number of volumes and give inclusive dates of publication and the date of the volume specifically referred to where this is not the first or last in the series (see examples (h), (i)). But if a work in several volumes is incomplete and still in the process of publication, the date of the first volume should be stated followed by a dash, and the date of the individual volume being cited should be added in parentheses after the volume number (see example (k)). In some instances (for example, if each volume of a set has a different editor) it may be more appropriate to give publication details only for the volume cited.

8. *Volume Number*: In a multi-volume work the number of the volume referred to should be given in small capital roman numerals, followed where necessary by the year of publication in parentheses (see examples (i), (j), (k)). It is very rarely necessary to insert 'vol.' before the volume number.

9. *Page Numbers*: If there is no volume number cited, 'p.' or 'pp.' should be inserted before the page number(s). It is customary to omit 'p./pp.' when the volume number is given (see examples (g), (i)), unless the page number(s) are also in roman numerals (see example (h)). If an entry relates to several successive pages, the first and last page numbers of the span should always be stated:

   pp. 278–309 (*not* pp. 278 ff.)

   If it is necessary to indicate a particular reference within a page span, the specific page number(s) should be given in parentheses (see examples (b), (g)).

   Note that 'folio', 'recto', and 'verso' are abbreviated thus:

   fol. 3^r, fol. 127^v, fols 17^v–22^r

10.2.3 Chapters or Articles in Books

Full references should be given as in the following examples:

(a) Martin Elsky, 'Words, Things, and Names: Jonson's Poetry and Philosophical Grammar', in *Classic and Cavalier: Essays on Jonson and the Sons of Ben*, ed. by Claude J. Summers and Ted-Larry Pebworth (Pittsburgh: University of Pittsburgh Press, 1982), pp. 31–55 (p. 41).

(b) Fanni Bogdanow, 'The *Suite du Merlin* and the Post-Vulgate *Roman du Graal*', in *Arthurian Literature in the Middle Ages: A Collaborative History*, ed. by Roger Sherman Loomis (Oxford: Clarendon Press, 1959), pp. 325–35.

(c) R. P. Calcraft, 'The Lover as Icarus: Góngora's "Qué de invidiosos montes levantados"', in *What's Past Is Prologue: A Collection of Essays in Honour of L. J. Woodward*, ed. by Salvador Bacarisse and others (Edinburgh: Scottish Academic Press, 1984), pp. 10–16 (p. 12).

(d) Luis T. González-del-Valle, 'Lo interpersonal en *Presentimiento de lobos*: un estudio de los modos de transmisión', in *Estudios en honor de Ricardo Gullón*, ed. by Luis T. González-del-Valle and Darío Villanueva (Lincoln, NE: Society of Spanish and Spanish-American Studies, 1984), pp. 141–53.

When a second item from a volume previously mentioned is to be listed, use the form:

(e) Eugène Vinaver, 'The Prose *Tristan*', in *Arthurian Literature* (see Bogdanow, above), pp. 339–47.

Similar conventions apply in the case of an article in an issue of a journal that has its own editor and a title:

(f)   E. Glyn Lewis, 'Attitude to the Planned Development of Welsh', in *The Sociology of Welsh*, ed. by Glyn Williams (= *International Journal of the Sociology of Language*, 66 (1987)), pp. 11–26.

The information should be given in the following order:

Author's name, exactly as it appears in the book (see 10.2.2, *Author*)

Title of chapter or article in single quotation marks

The word 'in' (preceded by a comma) followed by title, editor's name, and full publication details of book as in 10.2.2

First and last page numbers of item cited, preceded by 'pp.'

Page number(s), in parentheses and preceded by 'p.' or 'pp.', of the particular reference (if necessary)

A colon should be used to separate title and subtitle. For titles in English capitalize the initial letter of the first word after the colon and all principal words throughout the title (including the subtitle) (see examples (a), (c), (f)); for titles in other languages, follow the capitalization rules for the language in question (see 5.4 and example (d)). The titles of works of literature occurring within the titles of chapters or articles should be italicized or placed within quotation marks, whichever is appropriate (see examples (b), (c), (d)). If quotation marks are used within the title, they should be double (see example (c)), since single quotation marks will already have been used to enclose the title itself (see 8.3).

If a particular page within a chapter or article is to be indicated, the full page span should nevertheless be given in the first full citation and a reference to the particular page added in parentheses (see examples (a), (c)).

Reference to an article in a book which has previously been published in a journal should take one of the following forms:

Alfred L. Kellogg and Louis A. Haselmayer, 'Chaucer's Satire of the Pardoner', *PMLA*, 66 (1951), 251–77 (repr. in Alfred L. Kellogg, *Chaucer, Langland, Arthur: Essays in Middle English Literature* (New Brunswick, NJ: Rutgers University Press, 1972), pp. 212–44).

Edwin Honig, 'Calderón's Strange Mercy Play', in *Critical Essays on the Theatre of Calderón*, ed. by Bruce W. Wardropper (New York: New York University Press, 1965), pp. 167–92 (first publ. in *Massachusetts Review*, 3 (1961), 80–107).

The second form should be used if the collection of essays is more generally available than the individual journal (which may be old or obscure) or if reference is going to be made to several articles in the collection, thus facilitating the use of a short form for later references (see 10.3).

Other subdivisions in books, when separately cited, should be treated as seems appropriate according to this general pattern. Thus:

Troilus and Criseyde, in *The Works of Geoffrey Chaucer*, ed. by F. N. Robinson, 2nd edn (London: Oxford University Press, 1957), pp. 385–479.

Marqués de Santillana, *Infierno de los enamorados*, in *Poesías completas*, ed. by Miguel Ángel Pérez Priego, I, Clásicos Alhambra, 25 (Madrid: Alhambra, 1983), pp. 225–58.

10.2.4 ARTICLES IN JOURNALS

The first reference should be given in full in a form similar to that in the following examples:

(a) Richard Hillyer, 'In More than Name Only: Jonson's "To Sir Horace Vere"', *MLR*, 85 (1990), 1–11 (p. 8).

(b) L. T. Topsfield, '*Jois, Amors* and *Fin' Amors* in the Poetry of Jaufre Rudel', *Neuphilologische Mitteilungen*, 71 (1970), 277–305 (p. 279).

(c) Victor Skretkowicz, 'Devices and their Narrative Function in Sidney's *Arcadia*', *Emblematica*, 1 (1986), 267–92.

(d) J. D. Spikes, 'The Jacobean History Play and the Myth of the Elect Nation', *Renaissance Drama*, n.s. 8 (1970), 117–49.

(e) Robert F. Cook, '*Baudouin de Sebourc*: un poème édifiant?', *Olifant*, 14 (1989), 115–35 (pp. 118–19).

(f) Eduardo Urbina, 'Don Quijote, *puer–senex*: un tópico y su transformación paródica en el *Quijote*', *Journal of Hispanic Philology*, 12 (1987–88), 127–38.

(g) James Trainer, 'Sophie an Ludwig Tieck: neu identifizierte Briefe', *Jahrbuch der deutschen Schillergesellschaft*, 24 (1980), 162–81 (p. 179).

(h) Maurizio Perugi, 'James Sully e la formazione dell'estetica pascoliana', *Studi di Filologia Italiana*, 42 (1984), 225–309.

The information should be given in the following order:

Author's name, exactly as it appears in the article (see 10.2.2, *Author*)

Title of article, in single quotation marks

Title of journal, italicized

Volume number, in arabic numerals

Year(s) of publication, in parentheses

First and last page numbers of article cited, not preceded by 'pp.'

Page number(s), in parentheses and preceded by 'p.' or 'pp.', of the particular reference (if necessary)

The use of the colon to separate the title and subtitle in an article, the norms for capitalization within the title and subtitle, the treatment of the titles of works of literature occurring within the titles of articles, and references to particular pages within an article are, as the examples illustrate, treated in the same way as for articles in books (see 10.2.3). Note, however, that the page span of articles in journals is not preceded by 'pp.'.

Only the main title of a journal should be given. An initial 'The' or 'A' and any subtitle should be omitted. If the journal title is abbreviated to initials, full points should not be used (see example (a) and 3.4). The titles of journals should be abbreviated only when the abbreviation is likely to be familiar to all readers (e.g. *PMLA*), otherwise the title should be given in full. If there are to be several references to the same journal, an abbreviated title should be indicated after the first full reference (e.g. *French Studies* (hereafter *FS*)) or in a preliminary list of abbreviations. For the proceedings of learned societies, etc., the name of the organization should be italicized as part of the title (e.g. *Proceedings of the British Academy*).

The volume number should be given in arabic numerals, no matter what the style preferred by the journal (e.g. *Medium Ævum*, 58, *not* LVIII). The number should not be preceded by 'vol.'. If a journal has ceased and then restarted publication with a new numbering, this should be indicated by 'n.s.' (= 'new series') before the volume number (see example (d)).

If the separate issues of a journal cover an academic year rather than a calendar year, this should be indicated as in example (f). If the publication of a volume of a journal has been considerably delayed, the actual year of publication should be given in square brackets after the official year (e.g. 1983 [1987]).

Normally it will not be necessary to cite the month or season of publication or the part number of an issue of a journal, unless the part numbers are individually paginated, in which case the information should be given:

> Lionel Trilling, 'In Mansfield Park', *Encounter*, 3.3 (September 1954), 9–19.
>
> José Luis Pardo, 'Filosofía y clausura de la modernidad', *Revista de Occidente*, no. 66 (November 1986), 35–47.
>
> E. Iukina, 'Dostoinstvo cheloveka', *Novyi mir*, 1984.12, 245–48.

For the formulation to be used in referring to a journal article in an issue that has its own editor and a title, see 10.2.3, example (f).

10.2.5   ARTICLES IN NEWSPAPERS AND MAGAZINES

References to articles in newspapers or magazines require only the date of issue (day, month, and year), the relevant section where appropriate (e.g. 'Reviews section', 'section G2'), and the page number(s); volume or part numbers should not be included:

> Michael Schmidt, 'Tragedy of Three Star-Crossed Lovers', *Daily Telegraph*, 1 February 1990, p. 14.
>
> Jonathan Friedland, 'Across the Divide', *Guardian*, 15 January 2002, section G2, pp. 10–11.
>
> Jacques-Pierre Amette, 'Thé et désespoir', *Le Point*, 8 October 1989, p. 18.
>
> Carlos Bousoño, 'La ebriedad de un poeta puro', *El País*, 21 May 1989, p. 17.

Initial '*The*' or '*A*' is normally omitted when citing English-language news-papers and magazines, with the exception of *The Times*. The date of issue (with the month always in English) should be given between commas, not parentheses, and the page number(s) should be preceded by 'p.' or 'pp.'. Otherwise the method of citation is the same as for other articles (see 10.2.3 and 10.2.4).

10.2.6 THESES AND DISSERTATIONS

The titles of unpublished theses and dissertations should be in roman type within single quotation marks; capitalization should follow the conventions of the language in question (see 5.4). The degree level (where known), university, and date should be in parentheses:

> R. J. Ingram, 'Historical Drama in Great Britain from 1935 to the Present' (unpublished doctoral thesis, University of London, Birkbeck College, 1988), p. 17.
>
> Diedrich Diederischen, 'Shakespeare und das deutsche Märchendrama' (unpublished doctoral thesis, University of Hamburg, 1952), p. 91.
>
> Mary Taylor, 'The Legend of Apollonius of Tyre in Spanish and French Literature before 1500' (unpublished master's thesis, University of Manchester, 1977), pp. 45–47.
>
> James-Louis Boyle, 'Marcel Proust et les écrivains anglais' (unpublished thesis, University of Paris, 1953), p. 22.

Note that American universities distinguish between a master's 'thesis' and a doctoral 'dissertation':

> Barbara Jean Trisler, 'A Comparative Study of the Character Portrayal of Celestina and Other Golden Age Celestinesque Protagonists' (unpublished master's thesis, University of Oklahoma, 1977), p. 4.
>
> William Eugene Simeone, 'Sir Richard Fanshawe: An Account of his Life and Writings' (unpublished doctoral dissertation, University of Pennsylvania, 1950), pp. 166–79.

If a published abstract of an unpublished thesis or dissertation is known to exist, the information should be given:

> Jon Vaden Anderson, 'A Woman's Work: Feminist Tensions in the Victorian Novel' (unpublished doctoral dissertation, Texas Christian Univ., 1997; abstract in *Dissertation Abstracts International*, 58 (1997), 880–A).

10.2.7 PLAYS AND LONG POEMS

After the first full reference to the edition used (see 10.2.2), later references should be given as: *The Merchant of Venice*, II. 3. 10; *The Faerie Queene*, IV. 26. 35; *Paradise Lost*, IX. 342; *Aeneid*, VI. 215; *Samson Agonistes*, I. 819 (meaning, in each case, that the line is the first line of the quotation). It is unnecessary to give a closing line number when a sequence of consecutive lines is quoted. The form 'IV. 2. 210–23' should be used when a passage is referred to but not quoted. If there are substantial omissions in the lines quoted, the form 'IV. 3. 412, 423', meaning that the quotation begins at line 412 and that there is an omission before line 423, should generally be sufficient. The omission will also be marked in the text (see 8.6).

Small capital roman numerals should be used for the numbers of acts of plays, and for the numbers of 'books' and other major subdivisions. Smaller subdivisions (scenes, cantos, chapters, etc.) and line numbers are usually indicated by arabic numerals. Figures in references should be separated by full points (not commas), e.g. *Macbeth*, III. 4. 99–107.

10.2.8   THE BIBLE

References should be in the following form: Isaiah 22. 17; II Corinthians 5. 13–15. Note that books of the Bible are not italicized; small capital roman numerals are used for the numbers of books, arabic numerals (separated by a full point) for chapters and verses.

10.2.9   MANUSCRIPTS

Names of repositories and collections should be given in full in the first instance and an abbreviated form should be used for subsequent references. The degree of abbreviation which may be acceptable will depend upon the frequency with which a particular repository, collection, or manuscript is referred to. The names of manuscript collections should be given in roman type without quotation marks and the citation of manuscripts within collections should be according to the system of classification of the repository.

The following examples show the method of citation both for first and for later references. Note that, because of the danger of ambiguity, the abbreviations 'fol.' and 'fols' are preferred to 'f.' and 'ff.'. Note also the abbreviated forms for 'recto' and 'verso'.

First reference:	British Library, Cotton MSS, Caligula D III, fol. 15
Later references:	BL, Cotton MSS, Caligula D III, fols 17ᵛ–19ʳ
or:	Cotton MSS, Caligula D III, fols 17ᵛ–19ʳ
First reference:	Paris, Bibliothèque nationale, fonds français, 1124
Later references:	BN, f. fr. 1124
First reference:	Sheffield Central Library, Fitzwilliam MS E.209
Later references:	Sheffield CL, Fitzwilliam MS E.209
First reference:	Public Record Office, Home Office, HO 42/196
Later references:	PRO, HO 42/196

10.2.10 ONLINE PUBLICATIONS

10.2.10.1 GENERAL

Recent years have seen a rapid growth in publishing on the Internet (and on the World Wide Web in particular), and it has become more and more common to cite material published through this medium. Generally speaking, authors should exercise the same discretion in considering the quality and value of material published on the Internet as they would for material published by more traditional means.

It is not uncommon for Internet resources to change location on the server to which they were originally published, and even for them to be moved to a different server. Until a widespread system of persistent identifiers for information resources is adopted, Internet publications will often prove harder to pin down than their print equivalents.

As far as possible, follow the style used for printed publications as detailed in Chapter 10. Information should be given in the following order:

Author's name

Title of item

Title of complete work/resource

Publication details (volume, issue, date)

Full address (Universal Resource Locator — URL) of the resource (in angle brackets)

Date at which the resource was consulted (in square brackets)

Location of passage cited (in parentheses)

10.2.10.2 ONLINE ARTICLES

The following is an example of how to refer to an article published in a Web-based journal:

> Steve Sohmer, 'The Lunar Calendar of Shakespeare's *King Lear*', *Early Modern Literary Studies*, 5.2 (1999) <http://purl.oclc.org/emls/05-2/sohmlear.htm> [accessed 28 January 2000] (para. 3 of 17)

Take care to follow the format of the URL exactly and remember that addresses are case-sensitive. URLs should be cited in full, including the indication of the relevant protocol (http, https, ftp, etc.). Ideally the address should not be divided over two lines, but if this cannot be avoided, break at a forward slash and do not introduce a hyphen.

Give the date on which the relevant section of the resource was last accessed; this will ensure that the accuracy of your reference will not be undermined by any subsequent changes to the resource. Where page numbers or numbered paragraphs appear in the original document, they can be used to give the location of a citation. Do not attempt to infer page or line numbers from on-screen documents since they may vary according to the browser used.

10.2.10.3 ONLINE DATABASES

Online databases may be unique electronic publications, or they may provide collections of electronic versions of existing printed publications. For the latter, where possible, cite the details of original print editions as well as a reference to the electronic database in which they are incorporated (see also 10.1).

The first example refers to an article in an online encyclopedia:

> Kent Bach, 'Performatives', in *Routledge Encyclopedia of Philosophy* <http://www.rep.routledge.com> [accessed 3 October 2001]

The following is a reference to an individual poem included in a full-text online database:

> E. E. (Edward Estlin) Cummings, 'maggie and milly and molly and may' in *Literature Online* <http://lion.chadwyck.co.uk> [accessed 5 June 2001]

In the final example a complete book of poetry with its original pagination has been included in a database forming part of a larger resource:

> Davis McCombs, 'Star Chamber' in *Ultima Thule* (New Haven, CT: Yale University Press, 2000), p. 4, in *Database of Twentieth-Century American Poetry* in *Literature Online* <http://lion.chadwyck.co.uk> [accessed 20 September 2000]

10.2.10.4 OTHER SOURCES

We do not offer guidance here on how to cite references to e-mail correspondence or postings to newsgroups or mailing lists, or to exchanges in multi-user environments, all of which might be regarded as the equivalent of personal written correspondence. Documents on personal Web pages should be used with the caution appropriate to unpublished manuscripts.

For a detailed discussion of how to cite these forms of electronic publication, consult Xia Li and Nancy Crane, *Electronic Styles: A Handbook for Citing Electronic Information*, 2nd edn (Medford, NJ: Information Today, 1996) and *International Standard ISO 690-2: 1997* (Geneva: International Organization for Standardization, 1997).

10.2.11 RECORDINGS, FILMS, AND DIGITAL MEDIA

Reference to recordings of music or speech should incorporate the following items, as relevant, separated by full points: composer or author, title, artist, orchestra, etc., conductor, CD reference, e.g.:

> Johannes Brahms. Symphony No. 2. Wiener Philharmoniker. Cond. Carlo Maria Giulini. 435 348-2

Music of the Spanish Renaissance. Shirley Rumsey. 8.550614

Dylan Thomas. *Under Milk Wood*. Anthony Hopkins, Jonathan Pryce. 1992. CD LPF 7667

First names of composers, artists, conductors, may be omitted if not deemed necessary.

For films, the reference should include, as a minimum, title, director, distributor, date, e.g.:

The Grapes of Wrath. Dir. John Ford. 20th-Century Fox. 1940.

Names of artists may be given after that of the director. First names may be omitted if not deemed necessary. If a video reference is available, it should be added at the end.

References to material published on CD-ROM, DVD-ROM, or floppy disk should follow the format outlined in 10.2.1–10.2.3, but with the addition at the end of the phrase '[on CD-ROM]', '[on DVD-ROM]', etc., as appropriate.

10.3 LATER REFERENCES

In all references to a book or article after the first, the shortest intelligible form should be used. This will normally be the author's name followed by the volume (if applicable) and page reference:

McArthur, p. 62.
Chadwick and Chadwick, III, 72.
Elsky, pp. 42–46 (p. 43).

Sometimes, particularly in the case of editions of 'works' or collections of essays, a short-title form of reference may be more appropriate:

Boswell, p. 326.
Chaucer, Langland, Arthur, pp. 212–44 (p. 229).
Thomas Nashe, III, 96.

If no ambiguity is possible, the (volume and) page numbers should be given alone and preferably be included in parentheses within the text rather than as a note (see 9.2). Sometimes it may be necessary, for example when more than one work by an author has been cited, to repeat a title, in a shortened form:

McArthur, *Worlds of Reference*, p. 9.

If there can be no doubt which author is being referred to but more than one of his or her works has been cited, use the short title of the specific work followed by the page reference:

Worlds of Reference, p. 9.
'The Lover as Icarus', p. 12.

The expressions 'loc. cit.' and 'op. cit.' are too vague and should not be used. The term 'ibid.' should be used very sparingly and limited to those situations where there is no possibility of confusion, such as after a second reference which is separated from its predecessor by no more than four lines of typescript.

10.4   CITATION BY THE AUTHOR–DATE SYSTEM

The author–date system requires all bibliographical references to be placed at the end of a book, article, or thesis in alphabetical order by names of author(s) or editor(s), followed by date of publication. The form recommended for use in MHRA publications is as follows:

> Crystal, D. 1992. *An Encyclopedic Dictionary of Language and Languages* (Oxford: Blackwell)
>
> MacCaulay, D. (ed.). 1992. *The Celtic Languages* (Cambridge: Cambridge University Press)
>
> Grady, H. 2001. 'Falstaff: Subjectivity between the Carnival and the Aesthetic', *MLR*, 96: 609–23

In this last example, note the space between the colon and the page reference. The existence of a number of variables affecting nearly every component as well as typography and punctuation means, however, that there is considerable diversity of usage and authors should follow the form used by the publisher or journal to which they are submitting their work. The following illustrate two among many other possibilities:

> Crystal, David (1992). *An Encyclopedic Dictionary of Language and Languages*, Oxford, Blackwell
>
> CRYSTAL, D. 1992. *An Encyclopedic Dictionary of Language and Languages*, Blackwell, Oxford

Where there are two or more authors, we recommend the pattern:

> Ogden, C. K. & I. A. Richards

rather than 'Ogden, C. K. and I. A. Richards' or 'Ogden, C. K. and (*or* &) Richards, I. A.'. Editors should be referred to by the abbreviations '(ed.)' or '(eds)'. Note that some journals do not use quotation marks for article titles.

If the list includes more than one work by the same author, a long dash should be substituted for the name after the first appearance, e.g.:

> Posner, R. 1996. *The Romance Languages* (Cambridge: Cambridge University Press)
>
> —— 1997. *Linguistic Change in French* (Oxford: Clarendon Press)

If two or more works by the same author(s) have the same publication date, they should be arranged in alphabetical order of title and distinguished by adding letters after the date (e.g. '1998a', '1998b').

References in the text should give in parentheses the surname of the author, the publication date of the work, and, where necessary, a page reference, e.g.:

> Pidgins contrast with creoles, which are created when pidgins acquire native speakers (Crystal 1992: 302).

Variations include, among others, 'Crystal, 1992: 302', 'Crystal 1992, 302', 'Crystal 1992, p. 302'.

When the author's name is given in the text, it should not be repeated in the reference. In such cases, the reference either follows the name or, if this seems stylistically preferable, may come at some other point in the same sentence:

> Smith (1977: 66) argues that [. . .]
>
> Smith, who was known for his contentious views, replied (1977: 66) that [. . .]
>
> Smith regards this interpretation as 'wholly unacceptable' (1977: 66).

If unpublished documents are referred to, an abbreviated form of reference should appear in parentheses in the text and a separate list should appear at the end of the paper preceding or following the list of published sources (which may include unpublished theses and dissertations since they have specific authors). The items in the list should be arranged in systematic (e.g. alphabetical) order. The following examples illustrate, in the left-hand column, the abbreviations used in the text and, in the right-hand column, the full references:

BL Bib. Reg. 18 D III	British Library, Royal Books, Report to Lord Burghley on the western border, 1590
CRO, Probate	Cumberland Record Office, Carlisle Castle, Probate Records
NLS 6118	National Library of Scotland, Edinburgh, Armstrong MS 6118
PRO, HO 42/196	Public Record Office, Home Office, HO 42/196

10.5 CROSS-REFERENCES

Avoid, as far as possible, cross-references within an article or book. The page numbers in the printed article or book will not, of course, coincide with those in the typescript, and numerous references of this kind will therefore involve considerable extra work for author, editor, and printer, and will increase the possibility of error. Cross-references to pages can sometimes be avoided by giving references to chapters, sections, or notes, if the notes are numbered consecutively throughout each chapter or article: 'See Chapter 3', 'See Section 4.3', 'See Chapter 4, note 7'.

10.6   BIBLIOGRAPHIES

In an alphabetical bibliography the surname of the author or editor whose surname governs the alphabetical position will precede the forename(s) or initial(s). Do not reverse the normal order for collaborating authors or editors other than the first quoted. The following examples illustrate these points:

> Johnson, Thomas H., ed., *Emily Dickinson: Selected Letters*, 2nd edn (Cambridge, MA: Harvard University Press, 1985)
>
> Cook, Robert F., '*Baudouin de Sebourc*: un poème édifiant?', *Olifant*, 14 (1989), 115–35
>
> Fuentes, Carlos, *Aura*, ed. by Peter Standish, Durham Modern Language Series: Hispanic Texts, 1 (Durham: University of Durham, 1986)
>
> McKerrow, R. B., ed., *The Works of Thomas Nashe*, 2nd edn, rev. by F. P. Wilson, 5 vols (Oxford: Oxford University Press, 1958)
>
> Chadwick, H. Munro, and N. Kershaw Chadwick, *The Growth of Literature*, 3 vols (Cambridge: Cambridge University Press, 1932–40; repr. 1986)
>
> Strayer, Joseph R., and others, eds, *Dictionary of the Middle Ages* (New York: Scribner, 1982–89), VI (1985)

Where many of the books cited in the bibliography have the same place of publication (e.g. London or Paris), this may be abbreviated ('L' or 'P') or omitted, but there must be a general note to explain this at the beginning of the bibliography. The titles of frequently cited journals or series should also be abbreviated (without full points) and a list of these and the full forms given in a list of abbreviations:

> MLR   *Modern Language Review*
> YES   *Yearbook of English Studies*

The system of abbreviations employed in *The Year's Work in Modern Language Studies* is widely used in the fields of language and literature. If the bibliography covers other areas, a system of abbreviations generally recognized within the field should be used.

In a bibliography in list form, final full points after each item should not be used. In a long bibliography of foreign books the native forms of the places of publication are sometimes preferable; and if formal bibliographical descriptions of books are being given, the spelling of the place of publication should be as given on the title page. Whereas the length of an article will be clear from the citation of the first and last page numbers, the length of a book will not, unless the number of pages is stated. Since readers will often need to know whether to expect a pamphlet or a lengthy volume, the number of pages should always be stated in a bibliographical reference work (e.g. *The Year's Work in Modern Language Studies* or a volume in the series Research Bibliographies and Checklists). The number of pages should be stated after the date (or, if the author–date system is used, after the publisher); thus: '238 pp.', or 'xvii + 302 pp.', or '89 pp. + 32 plates', or '130 pp. + 12 microfiches'. It may also be helpful to include such information in a bibliography placed at the end of a book, article, or thesis.

Whatever system is adopted, it is essential to maintain consistency of styling throughout a bibliography.

PREPARATION OF INDEXES

11.1 GENERAL

All scholarly works longer than an article or short pamphlet need an index. Without it, the utility of a book or a thesis is seriously impaired: the reader is hampered in comparing one section with another; someone who read the book a year before and who wants to consult a particular passage may be unable to find it; and anyone who needs to search many volumes for a particular type of information, and who cannot realistically expect to read them all from beginning to end, will usually ignore the unindexed book. A very detailed table of contents will partially fill the gap, but there is no satisfactory substitute for an index.

Publishers and printers generally expect text to be submitted on disk or by e-mail. Indexes supplied in hard copy only (or on cards or slips of paper) are no longer acceptable. Indexing facilities within word-processing programs are not generally regarded as satisfactory for compiling anything but the most rudimentary index.

All indexers need technical guidance that is beyond the scope of this *Style Guide*. The Society of Indexers publication *Last but not Least: A Guide for Editors Commissioning Indexes* (free to editors and others commissioning indexes) gives information on the qualities and features that an editor will (or should) be looking for in an index.

11.2 INDEX ENTRIES

All scholarly indexes should include subject matter as well as names. It is much easier to compile a name index, but the reader of a book on America in the 1960s who needs to know about mixed marriages or monetary policy, and who finds nothing in the index between 'Miller, Arthur' and 'Monroe, Marilyn', will feel cheated, and with good reason.

Headings with a substantial number of page references should be subdivided: no one wants to look at all thirty-seven pages on which a person is mentioned in order to find the one that gives the date of birth. In general, avoid several levels of indentation, since this would lead to ridiculously short lines in a two-column index. Subentries may often be advantageously grouped in a small block of type. Remember that apparently identical words that have different senses, or represent different parts of speech, must not be grouped in a single entry.

For some types of work (e.g. biographies, critical studies) a single index is normally best. For others (e.g. catalogues of manuscript collections) several indexes may be needed.

One important distinction that experienced indexers make, and that experienced index-users expect, is between substantial treatment of a topic throughout several consecutive pages (shown as, e.g. '28–32') and passing references to that topic on each of several consecutive pages (e.g. '28, 29, 30, 31, 32'). Special features such as pages with illustrations or with substantial bibliographical references may be indicated by bold or italic numerals, but such devices should be used sparingly, lest they distract the user. For inclusive numbers, use the convention specified in 7.2, e.g. '301–03' (*not* '301–3' or '301–303') but '1098–1101' (*not* '1098–101').

11.3 THE INDEXER

The author of a book may be the best person to index it, but not necessarily so since the author may not be best placed to see it from the reader's point of view. Authors can make good indexers only if they are fully aware of indexing principles and can put them into practice. They may find that the task is more complex and time-consuming than they had realized and that engaging a professional indexer is a better option. In this case, the person engaged should if possible be familiar with the subject-matter of the book.

The Society of Indexers issues an annual directory, *Indexers Available*, both in printed form and on its website (http://www.socind.demon.co.uk). The Society's address is: Globe Centre, Penistone Road, Sheffield s6 3AE (tel.: 0114 281 3060; e-mail: admin@socind.demon.co.uk).

12 PREPARATION OF THESES AND DISSERTATIONS

12.1 GENERAL

There are great variations between universities in their requirements for the presentation and layout of theses and dissertations (we use 'thesis' as an inclusive term). The following general recommendations will be applicable to most theses, but should be supplemented by reference to the particular regulations of the university in which the thesis is to be presented. Candidates must, therefore, be in possession of a current copy of local regulations before a thesis is prepared for presentation.

All theses should now be produced on a word processor, even though local regulations may still allow for the presentation of theses produced on a typewriter. In what follows, therefore, the terms 'typing', 'typescript', 'typist', etc. refer to production by word processor. It is also taken for granted that recommendations in earlier parts of this *Style Guide* have been noted before preparation of the final typescript begins.

12.2 LENGTH OF THE THESIS

Local regulations vary considerably on the permitted lengths of theses and these regulations must be consulted and observed. The total length normally refers to the number of words in the main text and appendices, but usually excludes preliminary matter, bibliography, and index. If a text is being edited, the word limit normally excludes the text itself but includes all explanatory notes, glossary, introduction, appendices, etc.

12.3 PARTS OF THE THESIS

12.3.1 TITLE PAGE

The title should be a concise and accurate description of the content of the thesis. The title page should also give the full name of the author, the qualification for which the thesis is submitted, the name of the university in which it is presented, and the date (month and year). Many institutions have a prescribed form of words for the title page, which must be followed. If the thesis is in more than one volume, the number of volumes should be given on the title page of the first volume and later volumes should have their own title pages with the particular volume number specified. Pagination should normally be continuous throughout the volumes.

12.3.2 Abstract or Synopsis

An abstract should be included even on the rare occasions when local regulations do not require it. It is helpful to the reader, and it can be included in such publications as *Dissertation Abstracts International*. Local regulations are often precise and strict about the position, length, and form of the abstract. It is frequently required to follow the title page. Unless other regulations apply it should not exceed five hundred words. An accurate and concise summary of the organization and content of the thesis is normally required. The scope of the work undertaken, the method of investigation, the main divisions of the thesis, and the conclusions reached should all be described. The contribution made by the thesis to knowledge of the subject treated should be clearly stated, without either undue modesty or ostentation.

12.3.3 Table of Contents and List of Illustrations

Any preliminary sections following the table of contents, chapter and appendix numbers and titles, bibliography, and index should all be listed in the table of contents, with page references. Titles must agree exactly with their wording in the main text of the thesis. The listing of smaller subdivisions within chapters is useful, and if the thesis has no index it is essential. Such subheadings should be listed in full, and consistently throughout all chapters and sections. If a thesis is bound in more than one volume, the contents of the whole thesis should be listed in the first volume; each subsequent volume should begin with a list of its own contents.

A list, or lists, of illustrations, diagrams, etc. should follow the table of contents and should also give page references. For any full-page illustration which does not form part of the continuous page numbering of the thesis, this reference should be to the number of the page preceding the item in question.

12.3.4 Preface, Acknowledgements, Declaration

A preface may usefully follow the list of contents. General assistance that you wish to recognize — from supervisor, librarians, colleagues, grant-giving bodies — should be acknowledged here. Acknowledgements of specific instances of assistance are frequently better placed in a note at the relevant point in the text; acknowledgement of permission to reproduce illustrations, quotations, etc. should appear with the material concerned. When a thesis contains material that the author has already published (or used in an earlier thesis), this should be indicated in a preliminary declaration. If the thesis is based on joint research, the nature and extent of the candidate's individual contribution should also be defined here.

12.3.5 List of Abbreviations

Abbreviations (of titles, etc.) regularly used throughout a thesis should be listed, with a key, immediately before the first page of the main text (see also Chapter 3).

12.3.6 TEXT

Theses should be divided into parts, chapters, sections, and subsections as may be appropriate. The first chapter will normally take the form of an introduction, placing the thesis in relation to its general topic and to other work in the subject. Chapter titles and headings of sections and subsections should be factual, concise, and descriptively accurate.

12.3.7 NOTES

Unless local regulations specify otherwise, notes should be numbered in a single sequence throughout each chapter (or section), beginning a new sequence for each chapter, etc. For the placing of note references, see 9.3. The note reference numbers within the text should be typed above the line without punctuation (most word-processing programs will do this automatically). The notes should be placed at the foot of each page, in reduced spacing (use the footnote, not the endnote, function of a word-processing program). If, in exceptional circumstances, it is impossible to do this, the notes should be placed at the end of each chapter, section, etc. It is important to remember that, although a word-processing program will renumber footnotes automatically, most will not change references in the text (e.g. 'See note 3, above'), and these changes must be made separately by the author.

12.3.8 APPENDICES

Supporting information that is not suitable for inclusion in the main text or notes may be incorporated in one or more appendices. These, which should be appropriately titled, could include such material as tables, lists, transcriptions of documentary sources, and descriptions of manuscripts. They should never be used to include material of doubtful relevance or to avoid the constraints of the official word limit of the thesis (see 12.2).

12.3.9 BIBLIOGRAPHY

Every thesis must contain a bibliography, detailing all works referred to in the text (including notes and appendices). It should give full publication details according to the model given in 10.6 (or 10.4 if the author–date system is used). Some degree of subdivision may be desirable; in particular, manuscript and printed material, and primary and secondary sources, should be distinguished and it may be desirable to provide separate listings for works in different alphabets. Works not specifically referred to should not be included; if necessary, important items not cited in the main text could be mentioned in the introduction and therefore qualify for inclusion. Lists should normally be in alphabetical order by author, unless there is good reason to adopt an alternative order (such as chronological order for primary sources).

While the work is in progress, bibliographical details should be held separately from the thesis drafts, in computer files or bibliographical databases (such as EndNote, ProCite, Papyrus), or on card indexes (in which case, never include more than one item on a single card). If you adopt an author–date bibliography, take care to ensure that the numbering of items of the same date referred to in your text corresponds to that given in the bibliography.

12.3.10 INDEX

Although not always required by local regulations, the provision of an index of names and subjects is highly desirable, particularly for theses covering a wide range of material or concerned with the work of several authors. An index also is best held in card form until the latest possible moment; page references may then be added to cards when the final typing of the text is complete (see Chapter 11).

12.4 PREPARATION OF THE FINAL TYPESCRIPT

12.4.1 GENERAL

Adequate time must be allowed for checking and correction, especially when the final typescript is prepared by someone else. An entire thesis should never be given to a typist without some provision for checking while typing is in progress. Immediate examination of the first sections typed is essential so that recurrent problems and difficulties can be identified and prevented in later stages. Before any section of a thesis is handed over to a typist, all references and quotations should be verified and a thorough check made of the sequence of footnote numbers, both of the reference numbers in the text and of the numbers of the notes themselves.

Manuscript text should be typed at the earliest possible opportunity so as to avoid the loss of unique material. Thereafter, backup copies should be kept of all word-processed drafts.

12.4.2 PAPER, TYPEFACE, AND MARGINS

Unless local regulations specify otherwise, theses should be typed on one side only of white paper of A4 size and good quality. An easily readable typeface, such as 12 point Times, should be used. Margins should be 4 cm (1½ in.) wide at the left-hand side (for binding) and 2 cm (¾ in.) on the other three sides. Text should be fully justified, i.e. right and left.

12.4.3 SPACING

The text, preliminaries, and appendices should be typed in double spacing throughout. Single spacing should be used for inset quotations (see Chapter 8) and for footnotes; it is usually best for endnotes also. The bibliography and index will probably require a special tabular presentation; double spacing between items and single spacing within items is often a convenient layout here.

12.4.4 Pagination

Unless local regulations stipulate otherwise, page numbers should begin on the first page of the main text (following the preliminaries) and continue to the end, and should be placed at the top right of each page.

12.4.5 Headings and Subheadings

There is a great variety of possible divisions of a thesis: Are the chapters grouped into Parts I, II, etc.? Are the chapters divided into sections? Are there subsections? Is a structured system of numbering used, as in this *Style Guide*? This variety makes it impossible to lay down detailed rules. There are, however, two basic principles that must be observed, and both depend on the concept of a hierarchy of divisions (part, chapter, section, subsection, etc.). The first principle is that the hierarchy must be reflected in the space left between units: if there are parts, each part must begin on a new page and should have its own title page; chapters (and equivalent main sections) should always begin on a new page; sections should have more space between them than subsections. The second principle is that of typographical distinction of headings: the heading of a part must be more prominent than that of a chapter, which must be more prominent than that of a section, and so on. Word processors make it easy to centre headings or set them at the left margin, to use larger type, and to use small capitals, bold type, etc. in order to give the appropriate level of prominence. There should be more space between the end of a section and the heading of the next section than between a heading and the section it introduces.

12.4.6 Checking and Correction

The whole text should be thoroughly checked before the final version is printed. Quotations and references should again be checked against the originals (not merely against a previous version), note numbers should be checked, and the typescript should be read through at least once more. Remember that you are responsible for ensuring the accuracy of your thesis.

12.4.7 Cross-references

Unless a thesis is divided into many small subsections, page numbers will normally be essential for cross-references, which should be kept to a minimum.

12.4.8 Illustrations and Tables

Illustrations (especially photographic plates, and tables or large illustrations which have to be folded) may cause difficulties with binding; the advice of the binder should be sought at an early stage if illustrations are likely to be numerous. Local requirements for the mounting of illustrations should be carefully observed; a binding margin of at least the usual 4 cm (1½ in.) will be required. If possible, illustrations should be inserted in the thesis near the relevant portion of the text. There should be a separate numbering sequence for each category of illustration (plates, figures, tables, etc.). Numbers and captions should appear below the illustration. If an illustration or table has to be turned in order to be mounted on A4 paper, its left-hand side should be to the bottom of the page of the bound thesis. The process of obtaining several copies of an illustration can be surprisingly slow, and adequate time must be allowed.

12.4.9 NUMBER OF COPIES

Local regulations vary on the number of copies of a thesis to be presented and on whether one copy is returned to the candidate after the thesis has been examined. All copies, by whatever method they are produced, must be identical.

12.5 BINDING

Nearly every university requires that theses should be bound in boards; some require this binding to be delayed until after the thesis has been examined, others require binding to be completed before submission. Local regulations on the style of binding and on the lettering on the front board (if any) and the spine (usually at least the name of the candidate, the degree, and the year) must be observed. Binding delays are frequent, and adequate time must be allowed.

12.6 PERMISSION TO CONSULT AND COPY

Many universities now require the authors of theses deposited in their libraries to sign a declaration granting to the librarian the right to permit, without further reference to the author, consultation of the thesis and the making of single copies (for study purposes, and subject to the usual conventions of scholarly acknowledgement) of all or of parts of it. As always it is essential to be aware of current regulations in the institution to which the thesis is being submitted.

12.7 FURTHER READING

The following may be found useful:

Barzun, Jacques, and Henry F. Graff, *The Modern Researcher*, 5th edn (Boston: Houghton Mifflin, 1992)

Watson, George, *Writing a Thesis: A Guide to Long Essays and Dissertations* (London: Longman, 1987)

13 USEFUL WORKS OF REFERENCE

BS ISO 999: 1996: Information and Documentation. Guidelines for the Content, Organization and Presentation of Indexes (London: British Standards Institution, 1996)

BS 5261-1: 2000: Copy Preparation and Proof Correction. Design and Layout of Documents (London: British Standards Institution, 2000)

Butcher, Judith, *Copy-Editing: The Cambridge Handbook for Editors, Authors and Publishers*, 3rd edn (Cambridge: Cambridge University Press, 1992)

The Chicago Manual of Style, 14th edn (Chicago: University of Chicago Press, 1993)

Gibaldi, Joseph, *MLA Handbook for Writers of Research Papers*, 5th edn (New York: Modern Language Association of America, 1999)

—— *MLA Style Manual and Guide to Scholarly Publishing*, 2nd edn (New York: Modern Language Association of America, 1998)

Li, Xia, and Nancy Crane, *Electronic Styles: A Handbook for Citing Electronic Information*, 2nd edn (Medford, NJ: Information Today, 1996)

Merriam-Webster's Concise Handbook for Writers, 2nd edn (Springfield, MA: Merriam-Webster, 1998)

Ritter, R. M., *The Oxford Dictionary for Writers and Editors*, 2nd edn (Oxford: Oxford University Press, 2000)

—— *The Oxford Guide to Style* (Oxford: Oxford University Press, 2002)

14 PROOF CORRECTION

All corrections should be made distinctly in ink in the margins; marks made in the text should be those indicating the place to which the correction refers and should not obliterate the text to be corrected. An alteration is made by striking through, or marking as indicated in the table below, the character, word, or words to be altered, and writing the new material in the margin, followed by a concluding stroke (/). If several corrections occur in one line they should be divided between left and right margins, the order being from left to right in each margin; individual marks should be separated by a concluding stroke. Author corrections should be avoided at proof stage. However, if such changes are essential, authors should be aware that substantial additions or deletions will affect layout and pagination and the editor may insist on further changes within the page to compensate for the text added or deleted.

When checking final proofs it is necessary to ensure not only that each correction marked on earlier proofs has been made, but also that no further errors have been introduced during the process of correction. Line endings, page breaks, running heads, and page numbers should be carefully checked on final proofs. It is possible for errors to occur near the head or foot of a page during page make-up; therefore page proofs also should be carefully checked for this. It is often safer to check these points as a separate operation after reading through the proofs in the normal way.

Normally only matter to be substituted for, or added to, the existing text should be written on the proof. If, however, there are any problems or comments to be brought to the attention of the printer, they should be written on the proof, encircled, and preceded by the word 'PRINTER' (in capitals). Resist the temptation to give lengthy directions to the printer when a simple proof-correction mark will suffice.

The following table of proof-correction marks is based on Part 2 of *BS5261: Marks for Copy Preparation and Proof Correction* (London: British Standards Institution, 1976) and material from this publication is reproduced by permission of the British Standards Institution, 389 Chiswick High Road, London w4 4AL (tel.: 0208 996 9000), from whom complete copies may be obtained.

Group A General

Number	Instruction	Textual mark	Marginal mark	Notes
A1	Correction is concluded	None	/	Make after each correction
A2	Leave unchanged	– – – – – – under characters to remain	⟨✓⟩	
A3	Remove extraneous marks	Encircle marks to be removed	✕	e.g. film or paper edges visible between lines on bromide or diazo proofs
A3.1	Push down spacing material which has risen and printed between words or lines	Encircle blemish	⊥	
A4	Refer to appropriate authority anything of doubtful accuracy	Encircle word(s) affected	⟨?⟩	

Group B Deletion, insertion and substitution

Number	Instruction	Textual mark	Marginal mark	Notes
B1	Insert in text the matter indicated in the margin	⋏	New matter followed by ⋏	Identical to B2
B2	Insert additional matter identified by a letter in a diamond	⋏	⋏ Followed by for example ⟨A⟩	The additional copy should be supplied with the corresponding letter marked on it in a diamond e.g. ⟨A⟩
B3	Delete	/ through character(s) or ⊢———⊣ through words to be deleted	♌	
B4	Delete and close up	/ through character or through characters e.g. charaɟcter characcter	♌	

Number	Instruction	Textual mark	Marginal mark	Notes
B5	Substitute character or substitute part of one or more word(s)	/ through character or ⊢————⊣ through word(s)	New character or new word(s)	
B6	Wrong fount. Replace by character(s) of correct fount	Encircle character(s) to be changed	⊗	
B6.1	Change damaged character(s)	Encircle character(s) to be changed	✕	This mark is identical to A3
B7	Set in or change to italic	——— under character(s) to be set or changed	⊔⎵	Where space does not permit textual marks encircle the affected area instead
B8	Set in or change to capital letters	═══ under character(s) to be set or changed	≡	
B9	Set in or change to small capital letters	═══ under character(s) to be set or changed	≡	
B9.1	Set in or change to capital letters for initial letters and small capital letters for the rest of the words	≡ under initial letters and ═══ under rest of the word(s)	≡	
B10	Set in or change to bold type	∿∿∿ under character(s) to be set or changed	∿	
B11	Set in or change to bold italic type	∿∿∿ under character(s) to be set or changed	⊔⎵∿	
B12	Change capital letters to lower case letters	Encircle character(s) to be changed	≢	For use when B5 is inappropriate

Number	Instruction	Textual mark	Marginal mark	Notes
B12.1	Change small capital letters to lower case letters	Encircle character(s) to be changed	╪	For use when B5 is inappropriate
B13	Change italic to upright type	Encircle character(s) to be changed	⊔	
B14	Invert type	Encircle character to be inverted	↺	
B15	Substitute or insert character in 'superior' position	/ through character or ∧ where required	⌐ under character e.g. ⌐2	
B16	Substitute or insert character in 'inferior' position	/ through character or ∧ where required	L over character e.g. L2	
B17	Substitute ligature e.g. fh for separate letters	├───────┤ through characters affected	⌣ e.g. fh	
B17.1	Substitute separate letters for ligature	├───────┤	Write out separate letters	
B18	Substitute or insert full stop or decimal point	/ through character or ∧ where required	⊙	
B18.1	Substitute or insert colon	/ through character or ∧ where required	⊙⊙	
B18.2	Substitute or insert semi-colon	/ through character or ∧ where required	⁏	

Number	Instruction	Textual mark		Marginal mark	Notes
B18.3	Substitute or insert comma	/	through character	**,**	
		or ⋏	where required		
B18.4	Substitute or insert apostrophe	/	through character	⸜,	
		or ⋏	where required		
B18.5	Substitute or insert single quotation marks	/	through character	⸜' and/or ⸜,	
		or ⋏	where required		
B18.6	Substitute or insert double quotation marks	/	through character	⸜" and/or ⸜,,	
		or ⋏	where required		
B19	Substitute or insert ellipsis	/	through character	● ● ●	
		or ⋏	where required		
B20	Substitute or insert leader dots	/	through character	⦅● ● ●⦆	Give the measure of the leader when necessary
		or ⋏	where required		
B21	Substitute or insert hyphen	/	through character	⊢⊣	
		or ⋏	where required		
B22	Substitute or insert rule	/	through character	⊢⊣	Give the size of the rule in the marginal mark e.g. ⊢1 em⊣ ⊢4 mm⊣
		⋏	where required		

Number	Instruction	Textual mark	Marginal mark	Notes
B23	Substitute or insert oblique	/ through character or /\ where required	(/)	

Group C Positioning and spacing

Number	Instruction	Textual mark	Marginal mark	Notes
C1	Start new paragraph			
C2	Run on (no new paragraph)			
C3	Transpose characters or words	between characters or words, numbered when necessary		
C4	Transpose a number of characters or words	3 2 1	1 2 3	To be used when the sequence cannot be clearly indicated by the use of C3. The vertical strokes are made through the characters or words to be transposed and numbered in the correct sequence
C5	Transpose lines			
C6	Transpose a number of lines		——— 3 ——— 2 ——— 1	To be used when the sequence cannot be clearly indicated by C5. Rules extend from the margin into the text with each line to be transplanted numbered in the correct sequence
C7.	Centre	enclosing matter to be centred	[ ]	
C8	Indent			Give the amount of the indent in the marginal mark

Number	Instruction	Textual mark	Marginal mark	Notes
C9	Cancel indent			
C10	Set line justified to specified measure	and/or		Give the exact dimensions when necessary
C11	Set column justified to specified measure			Give the exact dimensions when necessary
C12	Move matter specified distance to the right	enclosing matter to be moved to the right		Give the exact dimensions when necessary
C13	Move matter specified distance to the left	enclosing matter to be moved to the left		Give the exact dimensions when necessary
C14	Take over character(s), word(s) or line to next line, column or page			The textual mark surrounds the matter to be taken over and extends into the margin
C15	Take back character(s), word(s), or line to previous line, column or page			The textual mark surrounds the matter to be taken back and extends into the margin
C16	Raise matter	over matter to be raised / under matter to be raised		Give the exact dimensions when necessary. (Use C28 for insertion of space between lines or paragraphs in text)
C17	Lower matter	over matter to be lowered / under matter to be lowered		Give the exact dimensions when necessary. (Use C29 for reduction of space between lines or paragraphs in text)
C18	Move matter to position indicated	Enclose matter to be moved and indicate new position		Give the exact dimensions when necessary

Number	Instruction	Textual mark	Marginal mark	Notes
C19	Correct vertical alignment			
C20	Correct horizontal alignment	Single line above and below misaligned matter e.g. misaligned		The marginal mark is placed level with the head and foot of the relevant line
C21	Close up. Delete space between characters or words	linking ⌒⌣ characters	⌒⌣	
C22	Insert space between characters	| between characters affected	Y	Give the size of the space to be inserted when necessary
C23	Insert space between words	⌣ between words affected	⌣	Give the size of the space to be inserted when necessary
C24	Reduce space between characters	| between characters affected	⌐	Give the amount by which the space is to be reduced when necessary
C25	Reduce space between words	⌐ between words affected	⌐	Give amount by which the space is to be reduced when necessary
C26	Make space appear equal between characters or words	| between characters or words affected	Ⅹ	
C27	Close up to normal interline spacing	(each side of column linking lines)		The textual marks extend into the margin

Number	Instruction	Textual mark	Marginal mark	Notes
C28	Insert space between lines or paragraphs			The marginal mark extends between the lines of text. Give the size of the space to be inserted when necessary
			or	
C29	Reduce space between lines or paragraphs			The marginal mark extends between the lines of text. Give the amount by which the space is to be reduced when necessary
			or	

MARKS TO BE MADE ON PROOF, OR PROOFS, AFTER READING

MARK	MEANING
'Revise' (and signature)	Correct and submit another proof.
'Revise and make up' (and signature)	Correct and submit another proof in page form.
'Revise and press' (and signature)	Make final corrections and print off without submitting another proof.
'Press' (and signature)	No correction necessary. The work may be printed.

Marked proof of text

(B9.1) =/   'A Provisional Hypothesis': Paternity or Pangenesis?   Y/ (C22)

(C21) ⊃/   by Ashley Taggert

(B22)   In this article I examine August Strindberg's play The Father   ⊔⊔/ (B7)
(1887) in relation to a particular biological debate current at
the time. To do so, it is first necessary to place this work
within a movement, naturalism, which self-consciously allied
itself with 'new' evolutionary developments. After all, only
nine months after the première of *The Father* (Strindberg) is   ⊔⊥/ (B13)
able to write, in a letter to Karl Bonnier of August 1888:
'Keep your tongue straight in your mouth, for now naturalism is entering the academy (not the Swedish); and it will
never be superseded as a philosophy until Darwinism, whose
logical consequence it is — is abandoned: Hoc est never!'   ⊙/ (B18.1)
For him, naturalism marks a radical break with the past.   S⟨/ (B1)
Moreover, its fate as a literary movement is indissolubly
linked to the theories of Charles Darwin. Should Darwinism
be discredited, then naturalism, 'whose logical consequence
(C3)   it is', necessarily would fall in its wake.

(C1)   It is worth stating at the outset what an extraordinary   ⊏⌐/ (C8)
aesthetic stance this is. Strindberg espouses evolution for
better or worse, appending the fate of naturalism to an
entirely scientific breakthrough. However, the tone of this
and other avowals attests to his fervent belief that there is no
question of 'worse', and that with Darwinism he has found,
in Zola's words, 'the instrument of my epoch'. Paradoxically,
those very qualities that made Strindberg a brilliant theat-
rical innovator (readiness to assimilate new ideas, the ability
to immerse himself completely in the latest discipline, a
fearsome subjectivity) made him a poor Prophet. The day   ≠/ (B12)
would come when he would feel himself quite capable of
abandoning naturalism and denouncing 'Father Darwin and
his son Haeckel', for reasons that lay well outside the sphere
of 'logic', 'philosophy', or scientific rebuttal. To complete
this last quotation: Father Darwin and his son Haeckel   ⅄/ (B18.5)
(B18.5)   knew nothing and wished to know nothing about the
resurrection; they only knew about birth and death. So   ⅄/ (B15)
pronounced is the later Strindberg's disgust that he gives

(B18) ⊙/

way to wild fulmination on what he now sees as the glaring absurdities of evolutionary theory. However, at the time of writing *The Father* this violent *volte face* lay many years in the future, and Strindberg remained a committed follower of Darwin

(C2) ⊤/

His naturalistic plays, of which *The Father* is an early example, embody a range of attitudes to the revelations of *The Origin of Species*. Characters are given speeches which quite ⊤ simply ⊤ could ⊤ not ⊤ have ⊤ been ⊤ written ⊤ in a pre-evolutionary context. It is not simply that they have overtones of Darwinian 'struggle', or the battle of wills.

ə̂/ (B4)

Beyond this, the playwright sets up oppositions, like that between Miss Julie and her servant, Jean, which take much of their symbolic force from a dialectic within evolutionary thought. How far sheer strength of will can make one stronger in the fight to survive is, and was then, question-able. Can psychological toughness and adaptability and

(B12.1) ≠/

,/ (B18.3)

(C27)

adaptability raise a humble species from its origins, or is it for ever condemned by an inferior genetic heritage? Or, to translate this into the language of class, can aspiration and intelligence ever be enough to transcend caste barriers?

ə̂/ (B3)

(B10) ~/
(C9) ⅃/

Paternity

(+ 2pts (C28)

Strindberg taps into a debate between the Lamarckian evolutionists, who believe that intention and the hard-line geneticists, who saw it all as a matter of physical (genetic) endowment. In order to understand the opposing forces embodied in *The Father*, it is first of all necessary to look briefly at the development of darwin's relationship with Lamarck, and to remember that for Strindberg, writing in the 1800s the key issues of transmutation, differentiation, reversion, and struggle were far from settled, and retained the power to disturb and outrage.

⟨A⟩/ (B2)

(B8) ≡/
(A4) ⊘?/

[1] *A Blue Book*, trans. by C. Field (London: Allen, 1913), p. 223.

) - 2pts (C29)

Ⓐ and volition have a role in elevating even the 'lowest' organisms to greater complexity,

15 INDEX

References are to sections

abbreviations, 3
  American states, 3.6, 10.2.2
  capitalized, 3.4
  currency, 7.4
  editors, 10.4
  endnotes, 3.3
  footnotes, 3.3
  full point, 3.4, 8.3
  italics, 6.2
  journal titles, 10.2.4, 10.6
  manuscript references, 10.2.9
  postal, 3.6
  quotations, 2.4
  references, 10.1, 10.2.1, 10.2.2, 10.3
  titles, 3.2
  weights and measures, 7.5
abbreviations list, 1.5, 10.2.4
  glossary, 1.5
  theses, 12.3.5
  titles of journals, 10.6
abstract, thesis, 12.3.2
academic qualifications, 5.7
accents,
  capitals, 5.6
  hyphens, 2.3
  see also diacritics
acceptance for publication, 1.2.1
accounts, number columns, 7.2
acknowledgements, 1.3.12, 1.5
  theses, 12.3.4
additions, 1.3.2.2
adjectives, capitalized, 5.1
adverbs, hyphenation, 2.3
alphabets, 1.3.3, 1.3.10
alterations, retyping, 1.3.2.2
amendments, minor, 1.3.1
American states, 3.6
  abbreviated names, 10.2.2
American universities, 10.2.6
angle brackets, 4.3
anthology of criticism, 10.1
apostrophe, 2.5
  truncations, 3.5

appendix, 1.5, 9.1
  theses, 12.3.8
arabic numerals, 7.2
  Bible references, 10.2.8
  journal volume numbers, 10.2.4
  lines of poems, 10.2.7
Arabic script, 1.3.10
art, works of, 6.4
articles,
  cross-references, 10.5
  journals, 10.2.4
  magazines, 10.2.5
  newspapers, 10.2.5
  online publications, 10.2.10.2
  references, 10.1, 10.2.3
  type for titles, 6.3
asterisk, general note to chapter, 9.3
author–date system citations, 10.4,
  12.3.9
author-typeset formats, 1.4, 1.5
authors,
  bibliography, 10.6
  collaborating, 10.6
  corrections, 1.3.2.2, 14
  final copy design, 1.3.1
  indexing, 11.3
  multiple, 10.4
  name in text, 10.4
  online publications, 10.2.10.1
  references to books, 10.2.2, 10.2.3
  references to journals, 10.2.4
  responsibilities, 1.2.3
  retained copy, 1.3.1
  revisions, 1.3.2.2
  typesetting, 1.5
author's preface, 1.5

Bible,
  italics, 6.3
  references, 10.2.8
bibliographical descriptions, 2.4
bibliographical details, 1.5
bibliographical references,
  abbreviations, 3.4
  author–date system, 10.4, 12.3.9

indexing, 11.2
bibliography, 1.5, 10.6
  explanatory note, 10.6
  note limiting, 9.2
  number of pages, 10.6
  spacing, 12.4.3
  theses, 12.3.9, 12.4.3
bold type, 1.3.3
books,
  alternative titles, 10.2.2
  cross-references, 10.5
  online database, 10.2.10.3
  order of parts, 1.5
  references, 10.2.2, 10.2.3
  subdivisions, 10.2.3
  titles, 5.4, 6.3, 10.4
  type for titles, 6.3
  volume numbers, 7.3
braces, 4.3
brackets, 4.3
BS5261: Marks for Copy Preparation and
  Proof Correction (1976), 14

camera-ready copy (CRC), 1.4.2, 1.5
capitals, 1.3.3, 1.3.15, 5
  accented, 5.6
  book titles, 5.4
  dignities, 5.2
  foreign titles, 5.4
  hyphenated compounds, 5.5
  initial, 5.1, 8.3
  journal titles, 5.4
  large, 1.3.3
  movements, 5.3, 5.5.2
  periods, 5.3, 5.5.2
  prehistoric eras, 5.5.2
  quotations, 8.1, 8.3, 8.4
  references, 10.2.2, 10.2.4
  small, 1.3.3, 1.3.15, 5.7, 7.1, 7.3
  subtitles, 5.4
  titles of people, 5.2
  titles of writings, 5.4
  unpublished theses/dissertations, 10.2.6
captions to illustrations, 1.3.12, 12.4.8
card indexes, 12.3.9, 12.3.10
CD-ROM references, 10.2.11
centuries, 7.1
  small capitals, 7.3
chapter,
  general note, 9.3
  references, 10.2.3
  theses, 12.3.6
chapter titles,
  camera-ready copy, 1.4.2.2

references, 10.2.3
roman type, 6.3
theses, 12.3.6
checking of typescript,
  final version, 1.2.3, 14
  theses, 12.4.1, 12.4.6
Chinese script, 1.3.10
classical names, 2.7
colons, 1.3.9, 4.2
  references, 10.2.2, 10.2.3, 10.2.4
colophon, 1.5
commas, 4.1, 4.2
  numbers, 7.2
  quotation marks, 8.3
comments,
  for editor, 1.3.2.2
  for printers, 8.4, 8.5, 14
  for typesetter, 1.3.2.2
compound words, 2.3
conjunctions, 10.2.2
contents list, 1.5, 11.1
  theses, 12.3.3
copy preparation, 1.3
  typing, 1.3.2
copyright, 1.5
  quotations, 8.7
corrections,
  marking, 1.3.2.2
  see also proof correction
criticism, anthology, 10.1
cross-references, 1.3.14, 10.5
  theses, 12.4.7
currency, 7.4
Cyrillic alphabet, 1.3.10, 2.8
Cyrillic script, roman numerals, 7.3

dashes, 1.3.5, 4.2
  long, 10.4
databases,
  bibliographical, 12.3.9
  online, 10.2.10.3
dates, 7.1, 7.2
  journals, 10.2.4
  newspapers/magazines, 10.2.5
  online publications, 10.2.10.1,
    10.2.10.2
decades, 7.1
declaration in thesis, 12.3.4
dedication, 1.5
definite article,
  journal title, 10.2.4
  newspaper title, 10.2.5
  place names, 2.6

desktop publishing (DTP) software, 1.4.3,
     1.5
diacritics, 1.3.10, 2.2
     see also accents
dictionaries, 2.2, 2.3, 5.1
     biographical, 10.1
digital images, 1.3.12
digital media references, 10.2.11
dignities, 5.2
disks, 1.2.2, 1.3.1
     references, 10.2.11
Dissertation Abstracts International,
     12.3.2
dissertations,
     preparation, 12
     published extract, 10.2.6
     references 10.2.6, 10.4
     see also theses
ditto, 4.2
divisions, hierarchy of, 12.4.5
dollars, 7.4
double-spacing, 1.3.2.1, 1.3.9, 12.4.3
drawings, 1.3.12
DVD-ROM references, 10.2.11

e-mail attachments, 1.2.2
editions,
     original, 10.1
     references, 10.1, 10.2.2
editors,
     abbreviation, 10.4
     bibliography, 10.6
     comments for, 1.3.2.2
     indexes, 11.1
     instructions to typesetter, 1.3.1
     references, 10.2.2
electronic publications, 10.2.10
electronic submission, 1.4.3
ellipses, 4.8
     omissions within quotations, 8.6
em rule, 1.3.5, 4.2
     2-em dash, 1.3.5, 4.2
en rule, 1.3.5, 4.2
encyclopedias, references to, 10.1
endnotes, 1.3.11, 9.1
     abbreviations, 3.3
era citations, 7.1
essay titles, 6.3
     references, 10.2.3
exclamation marks, 4.7
expository material, 9.1

facsimile reprint references, 10.1, 10.2.2
figures (numerical), 7.2

figures in text, 1.3.12
     numbering, 12.4.8
file transfer to printers, 1.4.3
films,
     references, 10.2.11
     titles, 6.4
final version, 1.2.1
     avoidance of over-design, 1.3.1
     checking, 1.2.3, 14
     revised, 1.2.3
floppy disks, references to, 10.2.11
footnotes, 1.3.11, 9.1
     abbreviations, 3.3
     checking, 12.4.1
     positioning, 1.3.1
     references, 10.1
     theses, 12.4.1
     word processor function, 12.3.7
foreign currency, 7.4
foreign expressions, 2.2
foreign language,
     italics, 6.2
     quotations/quotation marks, 8.2
     roman numerals, 7.3
foreign-language characters, 1.3.10
     accents on capitals, 5.6
foreign names, 2.7
     place names, 2.6
     Slavonic, 2.8
foreign titles, 5.4
foreign words in italics, 6.2
foreword, 1.5
founts, 1.3.3
     see also type size; typeface
full point,
     abbreviations, 3.4, 8.3
     long quotations, 8.4
     notes, 9.1
     parentheses, 4.3
     quotation marks, 8.3
     quotations, 8.3
     references, 10.2.7, 10.2.8
     short quotations, 8.3

Greek alphabet, 1.3.10

half-title, 1.5
hand-written copy, 1.1
hard copy, 1.3.1
     annotation, 1.3.1
     cross-references, 1.3.14
     special characters, 1.3.10
     tables, 1.3.13
headings, 1.3.1, 1.3.4

camera-ready copy, 1.4.2.2
hyphenated compounds, 5.5.1
punctuation, 4.4
section, 12.3.6
theses, 12.4.5
typographical distinctions, 12.4.5
word processors, 12.4.5
Hebrew script, 1.3.10
hyphenated compounds, 5.5
hyphens, 1.3.5, 1.3.9, 2.3
place names, 2.6

illustrations, 1.3.12
copies, 12.4.8
indexing, 11.2
list, 1.5, 12.3.3
numbering, 12.4.8
permission, 8.7
theses, 12.3.3, 12.4.8
indefinite article,
journal title, 10.2.4
newspaper title, 10.2.5
indents, 1.3.2.1
quotations, 8.4, 8.5
index, 1.5, 11
cards, 12.3.9, 12.3.10
entries, 11.2
features, 11.1
page references, 11.2
qualities, 11.1
spacing, 12.4.3
subentries, 11.2
submission, 11.1
theses, 12.3.10, 12.4.3
indexers, professional, 11.3
Internet publications, 10.2.10.1
introduction, 1.5
italics/italic type, 1.3.3, 6
copy produced on typewriter, 1.3.15
foreign expressions, 2.2
foreign words, 6.2
journal titles, 10.2.4
punctuation, 4.5
quotations, 8.1
stage directions, 8.6
titles, 6.3, 6.4

Japanese script, 1.3.10
journal titles, 5.4, 6.3, 10.4
abbreviations, 10.2.4, 10.6
references, 10.2.3, 10.2.4
journals,
article references, 10.2.3, 10.2.4, 10.4
page numbers, 10.2.4

publication date, 10.2.4
volume numbers, 10.2.4
justification, 1.3.2.1, 1.3.9
Koran, 6.3

Latin words, 6.2
learned society proceedings, 10.2.4
legal case citation, 6.3
letters, references to, 10.1
Library of Congress system, 2.8
line division for quotations of verse, 8.3
line ends,
camera-ready copy, 1.4.2.2
checking, 14
line spacing, 1.3.2.1
double, 1.3.2.1, 1.3.9, 12.4.3
single, 1.3.9, 12.4.3
theses, 12.4.3
literary works,
references, 10.1, 10.2.4
title abbreviations, 3.2
titles within article titles, 10.2.4

magazine article references, 10.2.5
manuscripts,
references, 10.2.9
typing, 12.4.1
margins,
proof corrections, 14
theses, 12.4.2
measurement, 7.5
The Modern Language Review, 2.8
monarchs, 2.7
roman numerals, 7.3
money, 7.4
movements, 5.3, 5.5.2
multi-volume work references, 10.2.2
musical composition titles, 6.4

names,
indexes, 11.2
references, 10.2.2
see also personal names; place names
newspaper article references, 10.2.5
non-alphabetic scripts, 1.3.10
notes, 1.3.11, 1.5, 9.1
checking, 12.4.1, 12.4.6
general to chapter, 9.3
limiting, 9.2
numbering, 1.3.11, 9.3, 12.3.7, 12.4.1,
12.4.6
position, 9.3, 12.3.7
references, 9.2
theses, 12.3.7, 12.4.1

typescript, 9.3
unnumbered, 9.3
see also endnotes; footnotes
numbering,
  notes, 1.3.11, 9.3, 12.3.7, 12.4.1, 12.4.6
  pages, 1.3.1, 1.3.8
  preliminary pages, 1.5
  subdivisions, 1.3.4
  text, 1.5
numbers, 7.2, 7.3
  see also arabic numerals; roman numerals

omissions from quotations, 8.6, 10.2.7
online publications, 10.2.10
  articles, 10.2.10.2
  databases, 10.2.10.3
  references, 10.2.10
order of parts of book, 1.5
ordinals, 7.1, 7.2
  roman numerals, 7.3

page break checking, 14
page ends for camera-ready copy, 1.4.2.2
page numbering, 1.3.1, 1.3.8
page numbers,
  checking, 14
  indexes, 11.2
  journals, 10.2.4
  references, 10.2.2, 10.2.3
  theses, 12.3.1, 12.4.4
paper size, 1.3.1
  camera-ready copy, 1.4.2.2
  theses, 12.4.2
paperback reissues, references, 10.1
paragraphs, 1.3.2.1
parentheses, 4.2, 4.3
  punctuation, 8.3
  references, 8.3, 8.4, 9.2
  roman, 8.5
  volume numbers, 10.2.2
PDF files, 1.4.3
periods, 5.3, 5.5.2
permissions,
  acknowledgements, 1.3.12
  quotations, 8.7
  thesis consultation/copying, 12.6
personal names, 2.7
  extensions, 5.2
  possessive, 2.5
  Slavonic, 2.8
  substitutes, 5.2
phonetic symbols, 1.3.10
photographs, 1.3.12

place names, 2.6
  of publication in references, 10.2.2
plates, 1.3.12
  numbering, 12.4.8
plays,
  acts, 7.3, 10.2.7
  quotations, 8.5
  references, 10.2.7
plurals,
  foreign currency, 7.4
  weights and measures, 7.5
poems,
  line numbers, 10.2.7
  long, 10.2.7
  online database, 10.2.10.3
  permission, 8.7
  references, 10.2.7
  subdivisions, 7.3
  titles, 6.3
  see also verse
popes, 2.7
  roman numerals, 7.3
possessive, use of, 2.5
postal abbreviations, 3.6
postal codes, 5.7
PostScript, 1.4.3
preface,
  book, 1.5
  theses, 12.3.4
prehistoric eras, 5.5.2
preliminary pages, 1.5
  numbering, 1.5
  roman numerals, 7.3
printers,
  file transfer, 1.4.3
  marks for, 8.4, 8.5, 14
printing, camera-ready copy, 1.4.2.3
professional qualifications, 5.7
proof correction, 14
  marking, 1.3.2.2
proof marks after reading, 14
proof-reading conventions, 1.3.2.2, 14
prose quotations,
  long, 8.4
  omissions from, 8.6
  from plays, 8.5
  short, 8.3
publication details, 10.1, 10.2.2
  date, 10.2.2, 10.2.4, 10.2.5, 10.4
  online publications, 10.2.10.1
  place, 10.2.2, 10.6
publishers,
  code specifications, 1.3.10
  copyright, 8.7

name in references, 10.2.2
punctuation, 4
  dates, 7.1
  ellipses, 4.8
  headings, 4.4
  italics, 4.5
  journal title abbreviations, 10.2.4
  long quotations, 8.4
  marks, 1.3.4, 1.3.9
  note reference numbers, 9.3
  notes, 9.1
  numbers, 7.2
  parentheses, 8.3
  quotation marks, 8.3
  quotations, 8.1, 8.3, 8.4, 8.5
  references, 10.2.2, 10.2.3, 10.2.7, 10.2.8
  short quotations, 8.3
  see also individual punctuation marks

quotation marks, 1.3.6, 6.1, 6.2, 8.1
  double, 8.3
  foreign language, 8.2
  full point, 8.3
  long quotations, 8.4
  poem titles, 6.4
  punctuation, 8.3
  references, 10.2.2, 10.2.3
  song titles, 6.4
  titles in books/journals, 6.3, 10.4
  titles within italicized titles, 4.5
  unpublished theses/dissertations, 10.2.6
quotations, 2.4, 8.1, 8.4
  checking, 1.2.3, 12.4.6
  copyright, 8.7
  direct, 8.1
  foreign language, 8.2
  indents, 8.4
  long, 8.4, 8.5
  mark to printer, 8.4, 8.5
  omissions, 8.6, 10.2.7
  plays, 8.5
  prose, 8.3, 8.4, 8.5, 8.6
  punctuation, 8.1, 8.3, 8.4, 8.5
  within quotation, 8.3
  short, 8.3
  spacing, 12.4.3
  spelling, 2.4, 8.1, 8.5
  theses, 12.4.1, 12.4.3, 12.4.6
  verification, 12.4.1
  verse, 8.3, 8.4, 8.5, 8.6

readers, 1.3.1
  proof marks, 14
recordings, references, 10.2.11

referees, 1.3.1
  proof marks, 14
reference works, 13
references, 1.5, 10.1
  abbreviated form, 10.1, 10.2.1, 10.4
  abbreviations, 3.4
  articles, 10.2.3
  articles in journals, 10.2.4
  author–date system, 10.4, 12.3.9
  Bible, 10.2.8
  books, 10.2.2, 10.2.3
  capitalization, 10.2.2, 10.2.4
  chapters, 10.2.3
  checking, 1.2.3, 12.4.6
  digital media, 10.2.11
  dissertations, 10.2.6, 10.4
  editions, 10.1
  electronic publications, 10.2.10
  films, 10.2.11
  forms, 10.2
  indexing, 11.2
  journals, 10.2.3
  later, 10.3
  magazine articles, 10.2.5
  manuscripts, 10.2.9
  newspaper articles, 10.2.5
  notes, 9.2
  numbers, 1.3.11
  online publications, 10.2.10
  page numbers, 10.2.2, 10.2.3
  parentheses, 4.3, 8.3, 8.4, 9.2
  plays, 10.2.7
  poems, 10.2.7
  publication date, 10.2.2, 10.2.4, 10.2.5, 10.4
  publication place, 10.2.2, 10.6
  publishers, 10.2.2
  punctuation, 10.2.2, 10.2.3, 10.2.4, 10.2.7, 10.2.8
  quotation marks, 10.2.2
  recordings, 10.2.11
  simple, 9.2
  in text, 10.4
  theses, 10.26, 10.4, 12.3.9, 12.4.1, 12.4.6
  unpublished documents, 10.4
  verification, 12.4.1
  well-known works, 10.1
  see also bibliographies; cross-references; publication details
renumbering, 1.3.8
reprints, references to, 10.1, 10.2.2
research, joint, 12.3.4
retyping, 1.3.2.2

revisions, 1.2.1, 1.2.3, 1.3.2.2
roman numerals, 7.3
  acts of plays, 10.2.7
  Bible references, 10.2.8
  volume numbers, 5.7, 10.2.2
roman type,
  quotations, 6.2
  titles, 6.3, 6.4, 10.2.6
round brackets, 4.3
running heads, 1.3.7
  checking, 14
Russian names, 2.8

saints, 2.7
scripts, 1.3.10
section headings, 12.3.6
semicolons, 1.3.9
series references, 10.2.2
series titles, 10.2.2
short story titles, 6.3
The Slavonic and East European Review,
  1.2.1, 2.8
Slavonic names, 2.8
small capitals, 1.3.3, 1.3.15, 5.7
  centuries, 7.3
  era citations, 7.1
  volume numbers, 7.3
smart quotes, 1.3.6
Society of Indexers, 11.1, 11.3
song titles, 6.4
sources, citation, 9.1, 9.2
spacing, *see* line spacing
special characters, 1.3.10
spellcheckers, 2.3
spelling, 2
  preferred, 2.1
  quotations, 2.4, 8.1, 8.5
square brackets, 4.3
  ellipses, 4.8
  journal year of publication, 10.2.4
  quotations, 8.4
stage directions, 8.6
statistical works, 7.4, 7.5
style, preferred, 1.2.1
style books/sheets, 1.2.1
sub-editors, 1.2.1
subdivisions, 1.3.4
subheadings,
  punctuation, 4.4
  theses, 12.4.5
  typographic treatment, 5.7
submission of copy, 1.1
  on disk, 1.2.2
  e-mail attachment, 1.2.2

electronic, 1.4.3
  initial, 1.3.1
subtitles, 5.4
synopsis of thesis, 12.3.2

tab characters, 1.3.2.1
tables, 1.3.13
  numbering, 12.4.8
  of numbers, 7.2
  permission, 8.7
  statistical, 7.4
  theses, 12.4.8
Talmud, 6.3
text, 1.5
  author's name, 10.4
  formatting, 1.3.9
  hyphenated compounds, 5.5.2
  major subdivisions, 7.3
  marked proof, 14
  minor subdivisions, 7.3
  numbering, 1.5
  references, 10.1, 10.4
  theses, 12.3.6
theses,
  bibliography, 12.4.3
  binding, 12.5
  checking/correction, 12.4
  contribution to joint research, 12.3.4
  cross-references, 12.4.7
  headings, 12.4.5
  hierarchy of divisions, 12.4.5
  illustrations, 12.4.8
  index, 12.3.10, 12.4.3
  length, 12.2, 12.3.8
  local regulations, 12.1, 12.2, 12.3.10,
    12.4.9, 12.5
  margins, 12.4.2
  material already published, 12.3.4
  number of copies, 12.4.9
  page numbers, 12.4.4
  paper, 12.4.2
  parts, 12.3
  permission to consult/copy, 12.6
  preparation, 12
  published extract, 10.2.6
  quotations, 12.4.3, 12.4.6
  references, 10.2.6, 10.4, 12.3.9, 12.4.6
  spacing, 12.4.3
  tables, 12.4.8
  text, 12.3.6
  typeface, 12.4.2
  typescript, 12.4
  unpublished, 6.3, 10.2.6, 10.4
  word limit, 12.3.8

title page, 1.5
  theses, 12.3.1
titles, 5.2
  abbreviations, 3.2, 10.2.4, 10.6, 12.3.5
  alternative, 10.2.2
  within article titles of literary works,
    10.2.4
  books, 5.4, 6.3, 10.2.2, 10.4
  capitals, 5.2, 5.4
  chapter, 1.4.2.2, 6.3, 10.2.3, 12.3.6
  descriptive, 6.4
  essay, 6.3, 10.2.3
  films, 6.4
  foreign language, 5.4
  hyphenated compounds, 5.5.1
  within italicized titles, 4.5
  italics/italic type, 4.5, 6.3, 6.4
  journal, 5.4, 6.3, 10.2.3, 10.2.4, 10.4,
    10.6
  musical composition, 6.4
  numerical, 6.4
  online publications, 10.2.10.1
  of people, 5.2
  poems, 6.3
  quotation marks, 4.5, 6.3, 6.4, 10.4
  references to books, 10.2.2
  roman type, 6.3, 6.4, 10.2.6
  series, 10.2.2
  short, 3.2, 10.3
  short story, 6.3
  song, 6.4
  typeface, 6.3
  of writings, 5.4
translators, references to, 10.2.2
transliteration, 2.8
truncations, 3.5
type size, 1.3.3
  camera-ready copy, 1.4.2.2
  theses, 12.4.2
typeface, 1.3.2.1, 1.3.3
  camera-ready copy, 1.4.2.2
  serif, 1.3.2.1
  theses, 12.4.2
  titles, 6.3
typescript, 1.1
  checking, 1.2.3, 12.4.1, 12.4.6, 14
  notes, 9.3
  theses, 12.4
  see also final version
typesetters, 1.3.1, 1.3.3

comments for, 1.3.2.2
editor's instructions, 1.3.1
text formatting, 1.3.9
typesetting by authors, 1.4, 1.5
typewriters, copy production, 1.3.15
typing conventions, 1.3.9
typographic style for camera-ready copy,
  1.4.2.2

underlining, 1.3.3
Universal Resource Locator (URL),
  10.2.10.1, 10.2.10.2
universities,
  American, 10.2.6
  local regulations for dissertations/theses,
    12.1, 12.2, 12.3.10, 12.4.9, 12.5

verse quotations,
  long, 8.4
  omissions from, 8.6, 10.2.7
  from plays, 8.5
  short, 8.3
  see also poems
volume numbers,
  books, 7.3
  journals, 10.2.4
  parentheses, 10.2.2
  references, 10.2.2
  roman, 5.7, 10.2.2
  theses, 12.3.1
volumes, publication dates, 10.2.2

weights and measures, 7.5
word breaks in camera-ready copy, 1.4.2.2
word processors, 1.1
  backup copies, 12.4.1
  digital submission, 1.4.3
  dissertations, 12.1
  file conversion, 1.3.1
  footnote function, 12.3.7
  headings, 12.4.5
  quotation marks, 1.3.6
  special character sets, 1.3.10
  theses, 12.1
words, definitions, 8.1
World Wide Web, 10.2.10.1

*The Year's Work in Modern Language
  Studies*, 1.2.1, 1.3.10, 2.8
  abbreviations, 10.6